HIKE

IRELAND

One WAY or Another

A Memoir by Scott and Jaynie Wall

Also, by Scott and Jaynie Wall

Walking the Camino de Santiago – An Ordinary Couple...On an Extraordinary
Journey

A wish that every day for you will be happy from the start and may you always have good luck and a song within your heart.
— Irish Blessing

Contents

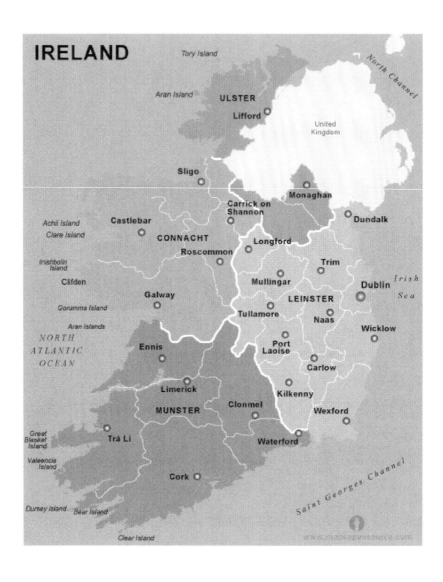

PROLOGUE

Our morning began with three options:

Option #1

Hunker down at the youth hostel located on the hillside and wait out Hurricane Ophelia. The risks being huge glass windows which could turn into lethal weapons, probable lack of electricity, and little food to choose from in the hostel pantry.

Option #2

Get on the paved road and hike several miles to the nearest village of Enniskerry and hope to find an available accommodation to wait out the hurricane.

Option #3

Get back on Ireland's famous Wicklow Way Trail and put in as many miles as possible before finding a town to spend the night.

THINKING ABOUT IRELAND

Sometimes, when multiple circumstances happen which point you in the same direction, you need to pay attention, right?

As Scott and I walked the Camino de Santiago in the Fall of 2016, we met Lou and Helen who told us stories of their visits to Ireland. The country had captured their hearts and they enjoyed hiking the "Ways" or waymarked trails all around Ireland.

After we returned home from Spain, I told Scott how important it would be in 2017 for us to attend a travel blogging conference. It would allow us to grow our blog, expand our opportunities through networking and meet other bloggers. Only a few weeks later one of the big conference hosts, TBEX announced their conference location for Europe in the Fall of 2017. It was to be held in Killarney, Ireland!

This was all it took for us to decide it was meant to be; Ireland would be our hiking destination for 2017.

We sincerely hope you enjoy our memoir. If it inspires you to hike in Ireland and paints a picture of the mountains, valleys, sheep, delicious food, plentiful beer and wonderful people, then we have done our job!

The format of our book will switch voices between Scott and I, with Scott chiming in for different parts of our story.

PRE-PLANNING

Scott and I decided to have our DNA tested through a popular company called 23 and Me. We knew Scott has some Irish heritage and I have some Welsh. You can imagine our shock when Scott's results came back 75% Irish and mine came back 24% Irish! I didn't even know I had an Irish ancestry. These results made us even more excited for our trip to Ireland.

Usually, I am the trip planner and Scott will give his opinions and input. As our trip approached, I was busy writing for our blog about our recent travels through Peru, as well as getting ready to publish our book, *"Walking the Camino de Santiago, An Ordinary Couple on An Extraordinary Journey"*.

This didn't leave me much time to focus on Ireland. Because of our recent ancestry discovery, Scott was highly motivated to do the necessary research on the many (40+) trails/ways Ireland has to offer. It wasn't an easy decision, Scott chose the two hikes which interested us most; The Dingle Way and The Beara Way. The distance of the hikes, as well as their location, were important deciding factors.

OUR INITIAL PLAN

O ur choice for the Ireland hike was the Beara Way. The trail is approximately 120 miles long and is based on the march of O'Sullivan Beare in 1603. Waymarked posts with yellow arrows and a tiny yellow man mark the entire route.

The history of O'Sullivan Beare is an interesting one and we couldn't help but think of the tragedy and lives changed by the march. O'Sullivan was the last independent ruler of the Beara Peninsula. To protect his people he took 300 children, women and elderly and hid them on Dursey Island (just off the coast of the peninsula). This was to protect them from the invading English. His plan didn't work, the English came to the island and massacred everyone, shooting them and throwing them from cliffs.

After the fall of Dursey Island, O' Sullivan Beare, with 1,000 of his people, began the 500 km march up the peninsula. This began on December 31,1602. The English forces fought them. After two weeks O'Sullivan arrived at County Leitrim with only 35 of his original 1,000. Many people had died in battle, while others had fled. Eventually, O'Sullivan and other Gaelic Nobility of Ireland, sought exile and made their way by ship to Spain.

The route of the Beara Way follows the line of the march.

Many tourists drive the Beara Peninsula along the southwestern coast of Ireland or choose to ride bicycles on the route.

Two mountain ranges run down the center of the peninsula; Caha Mountains and Slieve Miskish Mountains.

Scott and I plan to allow nine days for the hike, at approximately 15 miles a day. Along the route, there are sightseeing options. We can visit a castle, standing stones or explore a few of the nearby islands.

After our hike on the Beara Way, we plan to spend several days in Killarney. The TBEX Travel Blogger's Conference is to be held there and we plan to attend. It will be our first conference so we were excited to network and spend time listening to speakers on all topics related to travel blogging. After the conference, we are going to hike the Dingle Way. This hike is also in South Western Ireland, but farther up the coast than the Beara Way.

The Dingle Way is approximately 110 miles and takes an average of 8-9 days to complete. There are picturesque villages along the sea, as well as Bee Hive Huts and ring fortes. Slea Head is a must see for us with dramatic cliffs jutting into the wild Atlantic Ocean.

The rest of our month in Ireland is undecided. With more than 30 different, long-distance hiking trails in Ireland, we plan to explore several of them. The most frequented are Wicklow, Sheep's Head, Kerry, Dingle, Beara, Burren, and Western Ways. Over 4,000 km (2,500 miles) of trails, give us plenty of options. The Cliff's of Moher is high on our list to visit, as well as a visit to the city of Galway.

Scott and I have chosen ahead of time to not to rent a car in Ireland. We don't get along very well when we drive together, so that was an easy decision. Furthermore, we plan to hike most of the time and Ireland is known to have very convenient public transportation.

GEARING UP

Over time, we have narrowed down our favorite hiking gear. We have learned what fits comfortably for long hikes, as well as which clothing dries quickly. Quick drying material is essential, as we often hand wash our clothes on long, multi-day hikes.

One of the biggest changes to our normal gear we decided to make for Ireland was to invest in high-topped hiking boots. Usually, we both wear low-topped Hoka One-Ones. These are multi-terrain shoes with a ton of support, which act as a shock absorber and they save our knees in the long run. In Ireland, the trails will be more rugged and we will need to deal with rain and mud. I choose the Hoka One One Tor Tech Women's Mid and Scott chose the Merrell Men's Moab 2.

For the first time, we will wear gators over our shoes to keep them, as well as our lower legs dry. I'm not convinced we will even need the gators.

We learned some important life lessons while walking the Camino de Santiago. Even one extra pound of weight in our backpack can really affect our feet. For Ireland, I will pack more minimally than ever before; three pants, two long-sleeve shirts, two short sleeve shirts, a down jacket, a waterproof rain jacket with a hood, a buff, beanie hat, four pairs of socks, eight underwear and four sports bras. Scott's gear list is similar to mine. We need to keep our packs light!

When we left our house, my pack total weight without water was 10 pounds. I was happy and knew my feet would thank me later.

TRAINING

When we aren't training for a long hike, Scott and I practice yoga, go to the gym, play pickleball, ride local trails on our mountain bikes and take cycling classes. Sunday is always our hike together day. Some hikes are only a few miles long with the dog and some are 15 miles at higher elevations. Sunday is a special day for us. It's a good time to talk about the week ahead, discuss upcoming trips and make fitness goals.

In order to prepare for our long-distance hike in Ireland, we incorporated longer hikes with our backpacks about six weeks before departure. I also hiked alone with our dog, Joby, once or twice a week with my full pack.

We enjoy the Pacific Crest Trail, with a section only about 30 minutes' drive from our house. It's a good challenge and has higher elevations than we will encounter in Ireland. Scott and I felt strong and fully prepared for Ireland. One trail is just like any other, right? We had never hiked near the ocean, so we thought that it should be amazing.

SLOWLY, WE MADE OUR WAY TO THE START OF THE BEARA WAY

The first leg of our journey to Ireland was a red-eye flight out of Sacramento, California. I intentionally scheduled a nine-hour layover at JFK in New York. Scott had never visited New York City. It was the perfect opportunity for a quick stop and a nice way to break up the long flights.

We took the subway train from the airport into the city. It was Scott's first time on a subway and we weren't even sure how to get a ticket or pass to get on the train. Luckily, we watched other people and copied them after we looked at the train map. Scott was excited to see the sights. It's pretty cool to experience places in person you have only seen in the movies or on television. St. Patrick's Cathedral, and Rockefeller Center were the first places we saw. I showed him where the Today Show is filmed. Next, we boarded a hop-on-hop-off bus at Times Square to check out the city from a different viewpoint.

Later, we exited at China Town and walked to Little Italy for lunch. You can only imagine the smells of garlic and basil, along with fluttering flags in Italian colors up and down the narrow street. The pasta and red wine were delicious and we enjoyed people watching as we lounged in the sunshine after our meal.

Up next, we made our way by foot to the southern tip of Battery Park. Luckily, we found an empty park bench so we could relax and enjoy the view of New York Harbor and the Statue of Liberty way off in the distance.

After a short walk, we saw the monument for the 9/11 Memorial and One World Trade Center. We felt an overwhelming sense of loss for the tragedy that had occurred at this location. Unfortunately, we were unable to go inside the memorial as our time was up and we needed to get back on the subway and return to the airport.

The ride back was uneventful and not very crowded, so we felt relieved.

Back at the airport, we prepared to take our next flight to Dublin.

Plenty of research had been done so we knew there would be a bus leaving the Dublin Airport for the city of Cork. Upon our arrival at 5:30 a.m. we went outside and bought our bus tickets for about 20 euros each. The bus didn't depart for 30 minutes, which left us plenty of time to go back inside the airport to use the restroom and buy some snacks for our three-hour ride to Cork.

The ride was quiet, as only one-quarter of the bus was occupied. Keeping our eyes open was a challenge as we watched the rolling hills of green pass by. I think I got whiplash from falling asleep and waking up after nodding off every few minutes.

After our arrival in Cork that morning, we spent some time exploring the city. It was much bigger than we expected, which is usually the case for us every time we travel. Our host at the Crawford House B & B let us drop our backpacks off, but we were quick to learn that in Ireland, there is no checking into your room before 3:00 pm.

After walking the streets and admiring the River Lee, we chose a pub for our first official Irish breakfast.

Scott:

What is a traditional Irish Breakfast you ask? It's two fried eggs, two pork sausages, two slices of bacon, toast, baked beans, and black & white pudding. The black pudding is oats combined with blood sausage and the white pudding is ground up oats and pork without the blood, which makes it the white sausage.

At first, I liked the pudding but as the day went on, it left a lingering, unwanted taste in my mouth. I didn't like that. I still really enjoyed these big breakfasts.

After breakfast, we walked through the city streets until we found the Cork Visitor's Center. They helped us plan to take a bus the next morning to Glengarriff, where we were to begin our hike on the Beara Way.

The bus was scheduled to leave the next morning for a two-hour ride to the small coastal village of Bandy. Another bus was scheduled to come along to take us on to Glengarriff.

Scott and I enjoyed the rest of our day in Cork. It's a university town so there are many restaurants and pubs. There are boutiques for shopping and live music in many locations around the city. Scott's family ancestry has been traced back to Cork, so it was special to have that connection to the city.

A DAY IN TRANSIT

Early the next morning we took a taxi to the bus station where we bought our tickets to Glengarriff. We didn't need a reservation ahead of time, so we were happy. The bus was packed with people but still comfortable. We enjoyed the verdant hillsides and small towns as we passed our time all the way to Bantry. Being so excited to have arrived in Ireland, we were just trying to take it all in. Rain greeted us as we exited the bus in the small village of Bantry. We stopped for a moment to speak with a woman named Betsy, from Martha's Vineyard in the United States. On her back was a backpack similar to ours. She was a solo traveler and, like us, planned to begin her hike on the Beara Way the next morning.

The rain really began to come down, so the three of us popped into a pub for lunch. It was quite dark with wood paneling covering all the walls. It was warm, cozy and dry. There looked to be some locals at the bar so we took a booth next to the window. Betsy and Scott enjoyed a delicious seafood chowder, which was full of crab and fish, while I experienced my first of many cream of vegetable soups. I am a huge soup lover so this was a treat. The three of us tried some teas and coffee. I became educated by our server about my new favorite coffee. The proper way to order it is "Flat White", which is espresso with micro-foam, and steamed milk. It has a higher portion of coffee to milk and is absolutely delicious.

After lunch, our small group stood outside at the bus stop in front of the pub. The rain was pouring down and we were tucked up under the eaves the best we could be with our backpacks on. It was miserable and chilly, I quickly felt my limbs becoming stiff. The bus never came! Later, after speaking with some locals, we discovered the bus wouldn't arrive for 2.5 more hours!

Only slightly annoyed and confused, because we were still happy and excited to even be in Ireland, we walked across town to the Visitor's Center to learn about the area. The woman who worked there was delighted when she heard we were to begin the Beara Way. She took out a map of the Beara Peninsula and proceeded to circle the towns she liked along our route. There were only six or so and she circled them all! Then she went back and circled a few of the towns three times. We laughed and exclaimed that the towns with three circles must really be her favorites! She heightened our excitement for our hike. This woman was a wonderful representative of the area and we were just learning how much the Visitor Centers were to positively impact our travels through Ireland.

We continued to walk around town with Betsy in the rain, but it was really pouring. It's not surprising that we ended up back in the cozy, warm pub to dry off. Just in time for wine and beer. Betsy and I enjoyed a Spanish wine, while Scott tried the local stout. Two hours quickly passed as we exchanged stories of our travels.

Finally, the bus arrived. To our surprise, it was only a fifteen-minute ride! Had we known, we surely could have walked to Glengarriff in no time, or even called a taxi!

Scott and I had reserved a room the night before at the Glengarriff Park Hotel and Betsy walked across the street to the hostel. Glengarriff is a charming, quiet village of 800 people and is probably a lot of fun in the summer months.

We asked at the small grocery store if they had Wild Atlantic Way Passports. In these passports we could accumulate stamps for all of the areas we traveled through. Unfortunately, they didn't, but they said we could buy them at any post office along our route. We were hopeful that tomorrow we would find an open post office.

When the rain stopped later, Scott and I explored the town. We ran into Betsy and went in search of the sign which marked the start of our hike. Anticipation was building and we were all excited to begin the journey in the morning. We parted ways with Betsy, not knowing if we would meet again.

At the restaurant attached to our hotel, we asked the bartender if he had any ideas of places for us to spend the next night after we arrived in the town of Adrigole. He explained how it wasn't really a town, the only business being Peg's Shop. He sent us to the front desk where the helpful clerk called a B & B for us. She said, "Margaret, I have some walkers for you."

That is what they called hikers in Ireland. Hill walkers.

In a phone conversation with Margaret, Scott learned that after we hike over the mountain, we would end up at the highway and Peg's Shop. Margaret said Peg would call her and Margaret or her husband will come to pick us up and take us to their Bed & Breakfast.

At dinner Scott and I and talked about the day ahead. We had heard it was the most strenuous day of the Beara Way. I expected most of our hiking to be on flat trails in Ireland, and it was only ten miles. How hard could it be?

Scott:

After dinner, the lobby phone rang. It was Margaret, calling for Scott. She said, "Why don't you skip the hike over the mountain tomorrow, we will come to pick you up. It will be such an awful mess on the mountain. I don't know why you would want to hike in that."

Margaret seemed worried about us. I thanked her for her offer and said we would call her as soon as we made it to Peg's Shop. Talking to Margaret was like talking to your own grandmother.

That conversation made us even more nervous about what we were about to get ourselves into. However, we have hiked trails all over the world, steep trails at high altitude, as well as trails deep in the humid jungle. We anticipate a hike of ten miles over the mountain wouldn't be too challenging and we would be finished by lunchtime!

As we finished out our first evening on the Beara peninsula, I ate a huge steak and Scott enjoyed a fish burger. Live music played and we enjoyed the 70's rock and roll with an Irish spin to it.

BEARA WAY DAY 1

Glengarriff to Adrigole

Usually, Scott and I are early risers when we hike. Going into this Ireland trip, we knew things began more slowly in the morning than at home. There would be a big emphasis on breakfast, by the owners of the Bed & Breakfasts. We needed to eat a substantial breakfast because there would be no stops to re-fuel along most of our hiking route.

On our first hiking morning, Scott ate the traditional full Irish breakfast of eggs, ham, toast, sausages, and black and white pudding. I opted for the smaller version of ham and eggs. We enjoyed our coffee, then went back upstairs to our room to grab our backpacks and check out.

I was nervous about what was ahead for our day, our week, for that matter. It was also my first-time using gators over my shoes and ankles and I was questioning if I really needed them.

We quietly left Glengarriff and walked along a paved road which gradually took us uphill. It was so quiet, not a soul to be seen. Above town we passed by huge fields of green grass, only seeing a house every so often. It was a peaceful feeling, mixed with questions of the unknown.

We passed a rock outcropping thirty feet tall and were excited to see goats watching us from above. Little did we know, they weren't goats, but sheep; the first of hundreds we would see as we hiked in Ireland.

They stared blankly at Scott while he took their pictures as we passed by. The morning mist had burned off and the sun shined brightly. The humidity was different than we were used to back home in California. Our air is much drier and doesn't cling to the skin as dampness. We stopped often to drink water and take in the picturesque scenery. Gradually, we came into a huge, high valley, surrounded by mountains. It was absolutely gorgeous. In the distance, we saw a waterfall cascade down the mountainside.

A waymarker post with a little yellow man emblem attached to it was up ahead. It directed us off the road. We encountered our first fence as an obstacle to get over. It was equipped with a special ladder so we wouldn't need to open the gate and risk livestock getting loose.

Over the ladder we went with Scott taking pictures the entire time. "Really", I said, "are you going to take pictures of me crossing ladders the entire trip?"

He just laughed.

We quickly noticed there wasn't actually a trail to follow. Not a path, or even dirt single track. As far as our eye could see it was grassy farmland. The grass felt thick and sometimes there were shrubs and heather plants dotting the area. Way up ahead, we could see another post with a waymarker. Slowly, we climbed the steep, wet mountain. We made sure to keep the waymarker in our line of sight. For a while, we climbed a steep rocky section and stopped often to drink water and look back to check our progress. The views of the valley and the town of Glengarriff far below were breathtaking. With the waterfall in the distance, sheep here and there roaming the hillside, everything was so green it glowed.

We made slow progress as our feet sank into the wet grass. It was officially a bog hike. Thank goodness we had our trekking poles or we certainly would have lost our boots in the muck. The gators kept our shoes and laces halfway clean.

Step by step we hiked, an hour of climbing but only a small distance gained. Maybe ¾ of a mile. Time passed slowly through each muddy step in the bog. It began to get steeper, we could see what looked to be the top of the mountain. Way ahead and near the top were two slow-moving pops of color, people in blue and yellow. Other hikers were cresting the mountaintop.

Finally, after three hours of uphill, we reached the top of the mountain. Surprisingly, we had gone through much of our water. The weather being mild and humid must have contributed to our water consumption.

After a quick break, we were on our way again. Neither of us were much into long breaks, as it made it tough to get moving again. It didn't appear to be as wet or boggy at the top so I decided to eat a fruit bar as I walked. Bad idea! After about one minute of hiking without my trekking poles, I slipped, lost my balance and fell down on my entire right side in the mud. I didn't drop my snack though, so that was good! Priorities! Within the next half hour, I fell two more times. The mud on this side of the mountain was thicker, deeper and much more treacherous. I think the hardest part about falling down was the struggle with the poles to get myself on my feet again. Scott was usually right there to lend a hand, but that was an accident just waiting to happen. Luckily, the sun was shining and I was dressed in quick drying clothing.

We hiked around a small, clear lake and spotted people ahead who sat on a rock outcropping as they enjoyed the view while they ate their lunch. It was our friend Betsy from the day before. She introduced us to Friederike, a young German lady with long blonde hair and a huge backpack. They had become acquainted at their hostel the night before. Friederike was near the end of a few months stay in Ireland. She planned to get in some good hikes, before returning to Germany. We chatted a bit and enjoyed the view of the ocean far below. In the distance, there was a waterfall cascading down the mountain.

The four of us decided to begin our descent together. It was seriously muddy and a very slow process. We were always keeping one eye out for our waymarker. Mainly we followed a fence line between rocks since there was not any discernable trail to follow. It was fun to walk with the others, but difficult to make much conversation as we were all intent on our careful steps.

Once, Friederike fell down backward in a particularly deep muddy section, right onto her backpack. The expression on her face said it all, frustration, exhaustion and then worry as she remembered her cell phone was in the pocket of her jacket. She righted herself, checked her phone and, luckily, it was unharmed. We kept going and gave her a few minutes to gather herself before she joined us below.

Finally, we came off the mountain and walked down a paved road. There were signs of civilization here and there, a house or farm every once in a while. After three hours of downhill madness mainly in the mud, we arrived at the highway and Peg's Shop. What a relief!

Scott and I bought water because we had run out (this is very rare for us to ever run out of water) and we purchased small sandwiches from Peg for a late lunch. We explained to Peg about our situation with the Sea View Bed & Breakfast and she called Margaret right way.

"Margaret, I have your walkers here!" she said. My mind went instantly to the Walking Dead, a show about zombies they call "Walkers" we watch back home. I'm not sure why it triggered the thought, maybe because we considered ourselves hikers and not walkers.

Peg said it would only be a few minutes before our ride arrived. We said our goodbyes to Betsy and Friederike as they walked down the highway to a nearby hostel.

Scott and I were truly surprised at how small Adrigole was. We were thankful to be heading to the comfort of a B & B at the end of our long day. Six hours of hiking and only ten miles hiked.

Margaret's husband, Con, picked us up and delivered us to their B & B, about ten minutes up the hill. Their home was charming and overlooked the ocean far below. Margaret was all sweetness and took our wet boots, socks, and gators. She stuffed the boots with newspaper and put everything by the fire to dry overnight.

Then, she sat us down in the front room where we warmed ourselves and enjoyed tea and cookies.

Margaret and Conn's children were all grown up and lived elsewhere, so they rented out the spare bedrooms to guests. She explained how we were her last walkers of the season and they would be closed for Winter. We were so thankful they were still open. We had a nice, comfortable place to stay. Our room felt like we were sleeping at our Grandmother's house. I think she gave us the best room in the place. It was spacious with an ocean view.

After we cleaned up, Conn offered to drive us to the nearby pub and pick us up later. It was too far to walk and we were worn out. He explained how there was no food at the pub this evening because there had been a local youth futbol championship game and the final celebration had been at the pub. We were fine with a pint and a glass of wine; it doesn't take much to make us happy.

Conn drove us down the hill and dropped us off. The pub was busy. It was full of families celebrating after the game. Scott sipped on the local Murphy's stout and I enjoyed my white wine. We chatted about our day and watched people come and go. Day 1 of the Beara Way was certainly an adventure, and very scenic. We couldn't wait to see what adventure the next day would bring.

Scott:

We got hungry so I went to the bar to see about getting some kind of food, not necessarily a meal. Maybe a snack or a bowl of soup. While I waited, I noticed many pictures on the walls of youth futbol teams. The coach looked to be the same man as our bartender. When he came over, I asked if there was any food available. He said, "They've eaten me out of everything, there's not even a bag of chips left!"

I asked him about the pictures on the wall and he explained how he coached youth football for years. Instead of a snack, I ordered another ½ pint and Jaynie a glass of wine. It was going to be a liquid dinner tonight.

After a while, we decided we were ready to head back to the Sea View B & B. I went back to the bar to ask the bartender to call Conn for us. From a seat at the end of the bar, I heard a man say "No need to call, I will be their taxi. Just as soon as I finish my Guinness".

I turned to see an older gentleman smiling at me. He introduced himself as Eddie who lives next door to Conn and Margaret. He would be glad to drop us off and save Conn the trip.

We jumped into Eddies car and on our way up the hill, he told us stories of the area. When we arrived at the house, Eddie walked right in the back door and announced: "I've brought your walkers from the pub." After a few pleasantries and thanks from us, he was on his way home and we were on our way to bed for the night.

BEARA WAY DAY 2

Adrigole to Castletownbere

One thing I was enjoying about Ireland so far was how we were always able to sleep in. No one seemed to be in a huge rush to be up early, and we knew we couldn't ever check in to our next lodging until 3:00.

Scott and I met Margaret downstairs at 8:00 a.m. which was our pre-arranged time for breakfast. We enjoyed fried eggs, ham, toast, and tea. We tried the coffee option of instant decaf coffee crystals and to our surprise, the flavor was tasty!

Our time with Margaret and Conn was about to end. Margaret gave us our dry boots, socks, and gators. What a treat to put those on our feet as we sat on their porch overlooking the ocean.

Scott:

Our time with Margaret and Conn was short but special.

As we stood on the front lawn, ready to leave, Margaret told us that she hoped someday to walk over the mountain. It had special significance for her because her father had walked back and forth over the mountain to court her mother.

We said our goodbyes and Conn drove us to the point where we left off the previous day and would begin the day's section of the Beara Way.

It was 9:00 sharp as we began to walk along a paved farm road surrounded by fields of green. The weather felt mild, maybe 50 degrees Fahrenheit and it was slightly humid.

We walked for a short time and were then directed by our yellow man on the waymarker to go off-road and begin our climb up the mountain. Over the ladder, we went and slowly made our way uphill. Scott and I stopped often to turn around and appreciate the view. We began our hike on the road near the water and then ended up in a high valley. It was dotted with beautiful homes and grazing sheep. Another day of viewing waterfalls falling down the distant hillsides. The hike up was slow, but not as muddy as the previous day. After some time, we reached the top of the mountain. The top was very flat and covered in deep mud. The water must not have run down the mountain here. It took us at least 45 minutes to get through the wet mess.

Scott:

I was frustrated with our hiking or lack of hiking. Really it was bog walking. The steps were so slow because with each step we tried to make sure our boots stayed on our feet and didn't get pulled off. It was slow progress.

Scott's trekking pole became stuck in the bog water and he ended up losing his new rubber tip. I suggested he stick his hand down into the muddy water to retrieve it since he knew right where it was.

I watched him bend down and put his hand deep into the bog water, all the way up to his elbow, without finding the rubber tip. We just laughed and he went to a nearby creek to wash the mud off his arm. Luckily, he had a few spare tips for his poles.

We came across a ledge and spread before us were the downhill slopes of green grass as far as the eye could see. All the way to the ocean! The views were incredible. The sun was shining as we stopped to eat apples and nuts and drink our water. "This is exactly what I thought hiking in Ireland would be like, not muddy mountain climbing," I told Scott.

There was a dirt road for us to follow, with no mud. Sheep munched grass along the hillside. It was exactly what I love about hiking. Well, for about 15 minutes anyway.

As we walked downhill, we saw a couple of waymarkers which pointed in different directions. It was very unclear which way we should walk. There was no trail we could see or waymarker in the distance. So, we kept up our good pace and stayed on the dirt road.

Eventually, we passed a few farms and a sign which read WILD ATLANTIC WAY. We knew we must be on the right track since The Wild Atlantic Way is a 2,500 km coastal road specifically designed for tourists. Shortly thereafter, we arrived at the highway next to the ocean. We took a break and sat on a rock wall next to the road. It was time to analyze our map. We had definitely made a wrong turn at some point. We weren't due to be near the highway until we reached Castletownbere. From our rest spot according to the map, it looked like the Beara Way was farther back up the mountain. Neither of us wanted to hike all the way back up so we decided to follow the road for a while. This did present special challenges as the road was narrow and unlined and cars drive on the opposite side of the road than we are used to in California.

Scott:

I was pretty disappointed when I realized we missed the trail. Questions popped into my mind about how we could have missed the turn.

"It looks like there is a road which turns right and goes slightly uphill to join the trail. We only need to watch for the golf course so we know when to turn," Scott explained.

I was fine with that option, the only other choice being to walk the pavement all the way into Castletownbere. We kept our eyes open for the necessary landmarks, which were an art gallery and a golf course that were near the trail we wanted to take.

On and on we walked, I tried to stay positive and made sure to keep my eye out for a café or Bed & Breakfast at which we may want to spend the night later.

Unfortunately, we passed the golf course and never saw any kind of trail. There were no signs to direct us to the Beara Way. I thought, what next? This pavement walking was getting to me. I could feel the pressure of the weight of my backpack spreading out between my toes. Those poor pinky toes of mine, always the first to swell with blisters.

Eventually, we came upon a gas station. Perfect timing for a restroom and a can of ice-cold tea! A little bit of caffeine always put a pep back in my step.

Not long after our break, Scott and I walked into the charming town of Castletownbere, Ireland's hub for catching white fish! It sits right on Berehaven Harbor and in the distance, we could see Bere Island.

Our hike for the day was over, two hours of dirt hiking and two hours of pavement walking. It was interesting how my mood could shift from being euphoric at the top of the mountain to miserable resignation as I walked along the pavement.

Margaret and Conn gave us a couple of Bed & Breakfast recommendations in Castletownbere, so we walked through town and kept our eyes peeled. Being the end of September, it was very quiet. Many businesses were shut down or only open on limited days. We found the church Margaret mentioned with the long stairway beside it going up the hill. It led to another street above the church. There we found a pretty little B & B not far from the main street of town. A gentleman was in the yard and ended up being the owner. He said they had a room available for the night and took us inside to meet his wife. She was a bit taken aback by our sudden appearance, it being just after 1:00 in the afternoon. She exclaimed, "It's not 3:00 yet, you can't check in until then, I'm not even dressed!"

We could tell she was in cleaning mode and we totally understood. We left our backpacks and said we would return at 3:00.

Happy to have secured a room for the night, we went in search of a nice hot lunch. Lucky for us one restaurant in town was open. I enjoyed the best crispy fish and chips I've ever had and Scott devoured his chunky seafood chowder and crab sandwich. Lunch was superb! Of course, Castletownbere is known for its white fish and we were happy to sample the local fish.

Later, we properly checked into our room. It was a pretty spot and very clean, and being the low season, we got a water view room facing the island. A section of the Beara Way is on the island and we planned to go over after getting cleaned up in our room. While I showered, Scott ran our laundry down the street to be cleaned at the cleaners. It was time to deal with the blisters on my feet. They needed to be popped, drained and cleaned. For some reason, I couldn't find the safety pin I brought on the trip, just for this purpose.

Scott returned and we explained to the owner of the B & B how we wanted to take the ferry over to the island to walk for a while. Unfortunately, we didn't have time to get out there and explore and make the return ferry back. They were on winter hours now, which are a little bit more limited. Scott was disappointed, but we didn't make it a priority upon our arrival and didn't do the research to know the timetable. We both vowed to be smarter about our planning in the future. Another option we had was to go in the morning before we began our hike to the next town. We decided against that though, as the weather was supposed to be changing and we wanted to hike in the rain as little as possible.

After some quiet time in our room resting, we checked in on Facebook and sent texts to our family. Next, we went out to explore the town, pick up our clean laundry and find a grocery store. At the market, I was lucky enough to find sewing needles to help with my blister relief. We ran into our German friend Friederike, who was buying vegetables for her dinner at the hostel. She told us the story of her day:

Betsy and Friederike followed the trail of the Beara Way properly where we had turned off. They followed the sign even though it seemed to lead to a muddy, grassy hillside. It crossed the entire mountainside all the way toward Castletownbere. She explained how extremely muddy it was which led to more falling down in the mud. Sadly, they even saw a dead sheep. Ultimately, they decided to get off the mountain via the Emergency Exit Route. It led them to the highway and they walked the pavement the rest of the way into town. It took them about six hours total.

After hearing the story from Friederike, we felt better about missing part of the trail. Scott and I knew that in the future, we needed to be more careful and observant, just because a route appears easy we need to always see our route marker ahead.

The three of us made plans to walk together the next day. Betsy planned to spend time on Bere Island, so we probably wouldn't see her again.

After we said goodnight to Friederike, we walked through town and found an open pub. There were open seats at the bar and Scott and I settled in with a glass of wine and a Murphey's half pint. There was a group of ten or so people seated around a table in the middle of a raucous conversation. One man stood on top of his chair and started telling a story or a joke. We weren't really sure. Everyone was laughing so hard. They were having a lively time. Sipping our drinks, we tried to hear what was being said, they were speaking English but their Irish accents were too thick for us to decipher. Maybe it was a joke club, we wondered.

For dinner, we returned to the restaurant we had enjoyed at lunchtime to enjoy a delicious dinner and wine. I found the lasagna interesting, it was like a taco pie.

After dinner we walked around town, we felt happy with how the trip was going, despite the mud and getting lost. Our time in Ireland was progressing well, so far.

Back at our B & B, I focused on draining my blisters and bandaging my toes. We went to sleep early, as the next day would be a long one.

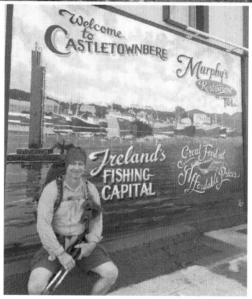

BEARA WAY DAY 3

Castletownbere to Allihies

Scott and I slept in as usual and then practiced our yoga. Breakfast was scheduled for 8:00 a.m. so we prepared our gear and planned to depart just after our meal. Our hosts at the B & B had previously owned a restaurant. We were lucky enough to enjoy a wonderful meal. I was so happy to have French Toast and American style bacon, which is thinly sliced and crisp, not a thick slab of ham.

Scott enjoyed the full, traditional Irish Breakfast, and we left the B & B well rested and with our stomachs full and content.

Before we met up with Friederike we stopped at the grocery store to buy more apples. Then at 9:00 sharp we met Friederike in front of the church to begin our day on the trail. It was quiet as we walked through town. Lucky for us we saw the post office was open. Scott went inside to buy a Wild Atlantic Way Passport for ten euros. The passport is a cool logbook for explorers. It encompasses 2,500 km of coastal road and there is much to see along the route. The postmaster stamped all of the places we had already been, so that was nice. Scott and I had collected stamps in our passports while we walked the Camino de Santiago. It's fun to go back and see a stamp and remember that special time. Each one held a unique memory.

As we left town, we gradually made our way uphill. Before we knew it, we came upon the Derreentaggart Stone Circle. This stone circle is one of 100 stone circles in Ireland. It was the first Scott and I had seen and we were excited. We walked around taking pictures and posing by the rocks. There are nine upright stones and three which had fallen over. It is said the circles were used for rituals and ceremonies and date back to the Bronze Age. They sat on a perfect location on a plateau looking out toward Bere Island.

Friederike didn't come near the circle or take a ton of pictures like we did. I asked her why and she explained she was being respectful of the sacred site. Then I felt bad as we had gone traipsing all over examining the stones.

Off we went again following the way markers with the little yellow man. Uphill we went. I knew we had a significant mountain range to get over midway through our day. The three of us enjoyed a nice pace and hiked well together. Sometimes, we took pictures and paused to look down at Castletownbere far below. Betsy was on our minds, as we could see Bere Island in the distance.

After a while, it became steeper. Of course, there was no trail, just grassy meadows. It became very foggy. We were socked in! The visibility was only 25 feet ahead. This made it a challenge to spot the way markers, but between the three of us, we made do. It helped that we had a general idea of the direction we needed to hike to get to the next town.

As we neared the top of the mountain range, it became incredibly windy. These were some of the strongest winds we had ever hiked in. I actually thought we may be blown over and off the mountain. Friederike fell down once when the wind caught her backpack like a sail. I gave her one of my trekking poles to use for stability. Using a pole for support made a big difference.

After about 30 minutes, we made it through the windy section and descended through a forest on a dirt road. Up ahead we climbed a steep gravel road for at least a mile. I was dying, and sweat just poured off my body. It was seriously humid. I took many French old lady steps (small steps, which go on and on, never stopping for a break).

Thank goodness there was no wind. It only seemed to blow across the top of the mountain range. As we climbed, I thought we were near the top as we rounded each curve, but we weren't. The fog was deceiving. At last, we came to a downhill and we were finished with our uphill climb for the day!

The three of us stopped for a snack break and took a few minutes rest. It seemed like we were overlooking more than the vast moorland, but the fog kept us from seeing more than just a few yards ahead. I imagined the ocean far below and even a small town, our destination later in the day.

The fog blanketed everything and muffled every sound we made and step we took.

Gradually, we descended the mountain on a paved road, and finally, the fog gave way to stunning ocean views. I knew it!

Ballydonegan Bay spread before us and we could see our destination ahead, the picturesque village of Allihies. The village is located on the tip of the Beara Peninsula and is known for its long history of copper mining. Allihies is a very clean village with brightly painted buildings in all colors of the rainbow. It must be a full-time job to keep those colors so vibrant and fresh!

The three of us entered town, situated a mile up from the ocean. A very strong and cold wind kicked up again, chilling us to the bone.

We said our goodbyes to Friederike as she went to her hostel. We wouldn't see her again as she had decided to go spend time in Killarney National Park. Thank goodness for Instagram though, as we can follow this kind, young woman from Germany to see where her adventures lead next.

The night before, Scott and I had made a reservation at the Sea View Guest House. It was unnecessary, as the town was empty. Our host was very kind and he showed us to our room with a beautiful bay view. We cleaned up and gave our feet a rest. It had taken us four hours to hike nine miles. Overall, it was an enjoyable day's hike, mud and bog free!

Next up was a stop at the coffee shop next to the Copper Mine Museum. We should have toured the museum, dedicated to copper mining in Cork County, but we were short on time. Scott had arranged with our host to have a taxi driver pick us up and take us to the cable car crossing at Dursey Island. The driver charged us 30 euros (about $34.00 USD) which included a twenty-minute drive each way and the driver would wait while we rode the cable car back and forth to the island. On our way, he told us some of the local history and pointed out different farms and family homes he knew. He dropped us off and agreed to wait for us until we returned. We bought our cable car tickets and were the only two people to get in.

A ride on the Dursey Cable Car was high on my list of activities to do in Ireland. We were both excited. The cable car was built in 1969. It is meant to transport people and livestock over the ocean to the island. Only two people live on the island now.

It was windy and very cold. The sky was gunmetal grey and a storm was due in that evening. My adrenaline was up as we crossed 825 feet above the ocean. The waves crashed into the cliffs below. It is a long-rugged shoreline. The experience frightened me but was exciting as well. How often do you get to ride a cable car over the ocean to an island? Scott was relaxed and moved around the cable car easily. He took a great video time-lapse, which brings back my quick pulse every time I watch it.

Once the cable car reached the other side, we knew we weren't going to explore the island. The weather was too miserable and we were tired.

No one joined us on the ride back, so it was just the two of us again. What an interesting and freaky experience. I can now check 'Cable car across the ocean" off my bucket list!

Our driver returned us to town. We were so thankful for the experience despite the poor weather.

We enjoyed lunch at a nearby pub and filled our bellies with vegetable soup and chowder. Later, we spent time in our room resting our feet.

Scott became bored and decided to walk the mile down to the beach in the freezing wind.

Scott:

I get restless pretty quickly. So, I bundled up and went down toward the beach. I didn't mind the wind. There's something nice about the crisp air by the ocean. I enjoy checking out new places and the walk was relaxing. After I made it to the beach, I put my feet in the water. It was my first time in Ireland touching the sea. I walked the beach for a while in search of seashells. Overall, this was a very relaxing afternoon for me.

I stayed bundled up in our room. Betsy was emailing with me. She was a day behind us on the trail. She planned to spend the night near Dursey Island and then jump ahead on the trail bypassing Allihies.

As I gave my feet some rest, I did my daily voice recording of our hiking experience. Voice recording was much easier than journaling. I could do it while I elevated my feet.

Speaking of feet, I didn't have any new blisters, so that was a good thing. Unfortunately, any wet bog hiking wouldn't allow bandages to stick. Thankfully, I brought along silicone toe tubes. I cut them down to size and slid them over any toes with blisters or hot spots. Toe tubes are the best thing ever! I should really be an ambassador for them because I love them so much!

Scott enjoyed his walk and spent time at the beach.

Later, we went out for a quick dinner and then early to bed, as we had another big day of hiking ahead!

BEARA WAY DAY 4

Allihies to Eyeries

D ay four began with us sleeping in, (this is rare for us and seems to be the ways things are going in Ireland), practicing yoga and then filling up with a big Irish Breakfast. After, we packed our belongings, thanked our hosts and were on our way at 11:00 a.m.

Scott:

Leaving at 11:00 a.m. is so different for me. I am usually awake and going for hours by then. This trip has definitely helped me slow down and relax.

The weather was predicted to clear up, but as we made our way uphill on the way out of town, the mist and rain drizzled upon us. The first hill we encountered was mud, maybe a livestock trail. We should have taken the road. Soon, the path joined the road and we were on pavement anyway.

Scott:

Jaynie thinks we walked in deep mud, but it wasn't. It was six inches of pure cow manure! It was so slippery and it definitely wasn't mud.

Just above Allihies, we passed the abandoned copper mine which was opened in the early 1800's.

The fog surrounded everything and we didn't get a good view. Luckily there were plenty of sheep to watch. As we walked by they stared back at us and grazed the hillside.

Over a mountain pass we went, which was not strenuous at all compared to the previous day's hike. By the time we reached the top, the fog cleared and we could see the ocean and a village far below. Our hike to Eyeries should only be nine miles. We felt so good. I wondered if we should pass Eyeries and double our mileage for the day.

Something interesting happens to our minds after a climb. It must be adrenaline or something similar. It was a feeling of happiness and motivation to keep going.

We began a slow descent and passed a small waterfall trickling down the mountain. Our positive feelings didn't last long as the waymarker led us off the road and onto the wet moorland. There was gorse (a yellow shrub) all across the hillside. We followed the waymarkers, but there was no trail or road any longer. Step by step we walked through miserable bogland. Water literally ran down the hillside we walked across. And let me make this clear, we didn't walk up or down, we went straight across.

In the unforgiving Irish countryside, we were present for every step. Each step in the mud, with one eye open, always alert for the next waymarker in the distance.

Thank goodness for our trekking poles. I think we said this every day. They saved us each day from falls in the muddy bog. Partway across the hillside, we came to beautiful cascading waterfall. Scott caught my picture as I was mid-jump across it. We plodded on, our afternoon suddenly moved in slow motion. Gone were thoughts of doubling mileage for a long day. With each step we tried to avoid the muddiest parts of the ground. Eventually, it didn't matter and we plodded on. We only had thoughts of a warm shower and hot tea ahead.

This hike in Ireland was so much different than our walk on the Camino de Santiago. We couldn't help but compare. On the Camino, it was one foot in front of the other each day. Our thoughts were free to wander and analyze life.

At last, we descended the long hillside and hiked around the mountain. So much for hiking to the village below. It wasn't even our destination! Gradually we went down and looked upon another bay. We followed the markers and soon walked through neighborhoods. Unfortunately, the waymarkers led us on a narrow path between properties. The mud was terribly deep and thick. It must be the way they lead their livestock to keep them off the streets. There was so much manure! After we finally arrived in Eyeries we felt exhausted and bummed out by our hike that afternoon. It seemed the Beara Way was not designed to lead us in a sensible, direct way from one destination to the next. It took us across miserable mountainsides for miles when we could have walked a dirt road. It also took us on disgusting livestock paths instead of city streets. After four hours and forty-five minutes of hiking, we made it nine miles. As we walked into town we were mentally exhausted.

Our previous host had graciously made us a reservation in Eyeries at the Foreman's House B & B. It was situated just above town, on a hill with gorgeous ocean views. We arrived wet and cranky but our hosts were so sweet and helpful. For about 70 euro, we enjoyed a big room, breakfast and one load of washed and dried laundry. They put our boots by the fire to dry overnight. Another nice touch was tea and cookies after we cleaned up.

The weather was so nice, we sat in the front yard and admired the ocean view. Our host made us a dinner reservation at the Bistro, the only restaurant open this late in the season.

Later, they dropped us off in town and we walked around admiring all of the colorful painted buildings. They even have a sign designating Eyeries a "Tidy Town".

Scott and I entered the Bistro at our appointed time and had our pick of seating. No one else was there. We weren't surprised since no one seemed to be in town, but it kind of threw us off since we had a reservation.

Service was impeccable and we enjoyed a dinner of vegetable soup, seafood chowder, salad and fish and chips. Of course, we enjoyed red wine as well. I was on the reward system and we earned that wine today. You may notice a common theme with our soup consumption. I love soup and can eat it every day. We enjoyed trying the different vegetable soups and chowders in each town. Believe it or not, the soups were different in each area of Ireland.

After dinner, we walked around town and enjoyed our first sunset in Ireland. It was gorgeous to see all shades of orange drop down into the ocean. Later, we stepped into a pub for a ½ pint of Murphys and a glass of wine. There were a few locals hanging out and one very drunk man. He was overly friendly to the point of being uncomfortable and he wouldn't leave us alone. We quickly finished our drinks and made the long walk up the hill toward our B & B. As we got closer we saw a sign at the town hall advertising a Bingo game, but it was for the following night. "Dang, I love Bingo, wouldn't that have been fun?" I asked Scott. He agreed.

Off we went to sleep back at Foreman's House, full bellies, clean, dry clothes and big hiking plans for the next day of the Beara Way.

BEARA WAY DAY 5

Eyeries to   ?

Scott and I woke with optimism bright and early. Our gear was clean and our boots dry. Rosario (our host) cooked up a delicious breakfast of eggs, ham, homemade scones and coffee. The big breakfasts helped sustain us for a good part of the day.

We said our goodbyes and they made the sweet offer to pick us up later in Ardgroom if we were unable to find lodgings. We weren't concerned though because things always worked out in the end for us.

Our path began right next to the ocean which was a treat. We were happy to hike along the water. At first, we took many pictures, but we knew rain was expected later so we needed to get a move on. Coulagh Bay was quite picturesque and peaceful. We saw cows and sheep and had to climb over a lot of ladders separating the grazing property along the ocean shore.

After two hours, the trail turned inland along a river and then finally a small ascent which allowed us to hike above and along Glenbeg Lake. The lake was smooth as glass and about a mile long. The lake was a known habitat of trout and salmon. There wasn't a soul to be seen.

High above the lake, we hiked on a narrow trail through the Glenmore Bog, which is an area of conservation. As you can imagine, it was slow going and very wet and muddy. After a while, we stopped to eat our apples, put our raincoats on and cover our backpacks to prepare for the rain. The sky was beginning to spit at us and it was only a matter of time before it began pouring in earnest.

After we walked two hours inland we came upon a road. We followed the pavement uphill for a time. The rain really came down and the wind whipped in every direction. I kept my head down and put one foot in front of the other. I didn't like to hike in the rain at all.

After a while, we turned off the road and up a steep path. We were miserable and happy to finally reach the top a few minutes later. Unbeknownst to us, we should have followed the Beara waymarker at the top of the hill and followed the trail over the mountain crest for one hour to our next destination of Ardgroom.

But at the top of the hill, Scott and I saw pavement ahead and it was going downhill. So, off we went, the wrong way, in the pouring rain.

We were on the Ring of Beara Scenic Highway. It was only a winding, one lane road and very quiet on this day.

The rain continued to pour down and the wind blew through us uncomfortably. We walked on and on. Eventually, we came upon a sign: 9km to Ardgroom. We were disappointed, freezing and exhausted.

Finally, we decided to stop a car and borrow the driver's phone, if only we would see a car! We hadn't seen one yet! We kept up a quick pace and fifteen minutes later a man drove past in a work van. Scott waved him down and thankfully he stopped to see what we were doing. Scott asked to borrow his cell phone to call our previous hosts The Foreman's to see if they could pick us up.

He was a sweet man that must have been close to our age, in his 40's, and told us to jump in. I sat in the front seat next to him (with a huge knife resting on the dashboard) and Scott sat in the back with several big water storage containers. There were cans of gasoline as well.

What a friendly man he was! He actually explained how he knew the Foremans and would take us right to their B & B.

But first, he needed to fill up the big containers with fresh water because a rabbit had drowned in his well and fouled the water.

He stopped and filled the barrel and then gave us a tour of the area. He slowly drove past his property, which had plenty of sheep and cows. Three of his cows were expecting babies any day now and he liked to check on them often. We passed by two of his sisters' homes, which were beautiful and usually rented out as holiday homes. He explained to us where we missed the trail at the top of the steep hill which would have taken us right to Ardgroom and made for a much shorter day.

In no time he delivered us back to the Foreman's B & B in Eyeries. We were appreciative of this kind man and thankful we had the fortune to meet him.

We checked in with our hosts, who were quite surprised to see us looking like drowned rats. The hiking boots went by the fire and the clothing hung from the radiator to dry. After our showers, we enjoyed cookies and tea and relaxed for a while. What a crazy day!

Although, it wasn't over yet. I had an email from Betsy, who we hiked with earlier on the Beara Way. She had arrived in Eyeries! We arranged to meet for dinner at the Bistro. Rosario, our host was quick to make us a dinner reservation and off we went!

The three of us spent a leisurely evening drinking red wine, eating chowder and fish and chips. We exchanged stories of our experiences the past few days.

Betsy planned to leave in the morning to walk the same route we had walked today. Scott advised her to watch for the right-hand turn we missed. Also, we advised her to skip an hour of the shoreline walk and begin at the other end of town. All things combined would give her a shorter hike to Ardgroom. Plus, she didn't plan to stay in Ardgroom. She planned to hike the next section like we were.

We made arrangements to meet up in two days' time so we could finish the Beara Way together. After saying our goodbyes, we made our way back towards the Foreman's B & B.

Just before the B & B, we saw the Bingo Hall. It was all lit up and there were cars everywhere. The sign said 8:30 Bingo. It was 8:15!

I exclaimed, "We have to go play Bingo, Scott!"

Just then a woman pulled up next to us in her car and parked. We talked with her for a few minutes and she encouraged us to play. "Come join us!" she said.

So, we did!

The three of us walked into the packed Bingo Hall. There must have been 60 people who turned to look at us. They were sweet and welcoming. We bought books of Bingo cards for seven euros each.

Scott and I were directed to the front corner of the room and sat at a table with four women. They explained the rules and how to play. This Bingo game was not Bingo as we know it back home in California. There weren't any letters, only rows of numbers up to 99. And, when you have a complete line, you don't yell out "Bingo!" You yell "Check!"

Scott quickly realized he was one of only three men in the entire room. Good thing he was a fan of Bingo!

Scott:

Jaynie is great about trying things that I usually wouldn't do. Joining a Bingo game wasn't in my plans but I try to stay open-minded. We had a fun evening and everyone was so friendly. What a great unplanned evening!

Our table was lucky, with lots of winning going on the entire night. I even won two games. The ladies kept an eye on our cards as well as their own. One woman yelled "check" for my cards before I even saw I had a Bingo myself.

At intermission, we snacked on delicious cake and tea. Overall, we enjoyed a wonderful evening.

Later, after we returned to our B & B, we found out Rosario, our host usually plays Bingo as well. But on this evening she had other plans.

What a crazy day! As we headed to bed we were so grateful that the people of Ireland continuously demonstrated their kindness to us over and over again. We were exhausted and would sleep well in our comfortable bed.

Scott:

I was annoyed that we had gotten lost again on the Beara Way and missed our turn. I was going to make sure we didn't make any wrong turns in the days to come.

BEARA WAY DAY 6

Ardgroom to Lauragh

The sun shined gloriously as we woke up, we were full of optimism for another day.

Scott and I enjoyed our Irish Breakfast. Scott had the full, while I had the smaller version of eggs and ham. It was a bit of a challenge for me to get used to eating such a big breakfast as soon as I woke up and then to go hike for hours with a full stomach.

Our host gave us a lift to the village of Ardgroom, and we began the next section of the Beara Way.

We followed the waymarkers with the little yellow man for about an hour along a quiet roadway. We seldom saw a soul. However, a cute black puppy came out of nowhere and followed us for a while.

Scott noticed a sign pointing off the road. Good thing he saw it! I would have kept walking down the road.

We climbed over the first of many livestock ladders for the day. Then, uphill we climbed, one step after another in thick, wet grass.

The higher we ascended the better the views became. There were very few trees to block the view, only low shrubs, and rocks. Far below was the Kenmare River Estuary. What a glorious day! It amazed us how day to day and minute to minute, the weather in Ireland changed so quickly. While the sun shined the hills glowed green.

Once we reached the top of the climb it was easier to walk. We hiked along a higher ridge on the mountain for a while. Far ahead, we saw a couple hiking in our direction. When our paths met we stopped to speak with them for a few minutes. They were from Germany and taking a day hike to do some sightseeing. They let us know there was a stone circle ahead and to keep our eye out for it.

Off we went again. Scott and I had a tough time getting from waymarker to waymarker in this section. We backtracked a couple of times to stay on track.

Eventually, we came to the stone circle and took a few pictures. These stones were placed during the 11th Century.

We enjoyed our hike in the sunshine. The temperature was in the 60's (f) and no jackets were needed.

Slowly, we made our way downhill and into a densely wooded forest. The trees were packed closely together and blocked our line of sight. Good thing the trail was obvious, although narrow in some spots. Green shaggy moss covered the rocks and tree trunks. It felt like the perfect home for a fairy or hobbit.

Suddenly, it became very gloomy and began to rain. Quickly, we covered our backpacks and put on our rain jackets. After about ten minutes we came out on the other side of the forest and the sun once again shined down on us. The rain stopped and there wasn't a cloud in the sky!

For a long time, we walked along a quiet paved road. Eventually, we arrived at an important junction. We left the Beara Way at this point and walked two more miles down the road towards the water. Our plan was to see if there was a room available at the Guest House attached to Helen's Bar. This was recommended to us by the ladies at Bingo. They raved about how the attached restaurant was the best for seafood.

Our feet were sore and tired. A long walk on pavement takes its toll, especially at the end of the day.

There was a room available (ocean view) and we happily cleaned up. We went downstairs to the restaurant for our typical lunch of seafood chowder and vegetable soup, our standard fare. It was delicious and warmed our bellies.

Our day's hike had taken 4.5 hours and was ten miles long. Every day we were surprised at how long it took to go so few miles.

After lunch, we spent time in our room resting with our feet up. We enjoyed the view of Kilmackillogue harbor and the mountains we had crossed in the distance.

Scott and I write a travel blog and posted a few daily pictures to the Backpacking Detours Facebook page.

Later, we went outside to check out the pier and enjoy the sunset. The wind was strong and cold as it came off the water. I didn't last long and left Scott on the pier to get warm in the pub with a glass of wine. As I entered the restaurant, I saw a big metal rectangle all lit up hanging from the ceiling. I went to it and moved my chair below it to capture some of the warmth. It seemed to be some kind of hanging heater.

I sipped my red wine and relaxed while watching locals and tourists alike enjoy their meals.

Scott joined me a few minutes later and the first thing he said was "Why are you sitting underneath the bug zapper?"

"Oh, no," I said as I quickly jumped up and moved my chair. We both laughed when I said, "I thought it was a heater."

Dinner was hectic in the restaurant. We took our time and watched the locals come and go. Scott ordered the seafood platter. He was in heaven with crab legs, salmon, smoked salmon, clams and crab salad.

I, on the other hand, was not impressed with my fish and chips, as they were too thickly battered and deep fried for my taste. I was spoiled by all of the delicious seafood and was starting to get picky.

After a leisurely dinner and more wine, we were off to bed.

Another good night's sleep for us and then our last day on the Beara Way lay ahead. We felt unhappy our Beara journey was almost over.

BEARA WAY DAY 7

Lauragh to Kenmare

Scott and I were at the breakfast table at 8:20 a.m. sharp. It was the exact time we pre-arranged with Helen to have our meal. At 8:50 she was to drive us back up to the main road intersection so we could pick up where we left off on the Beara Way.

Betsy and I had emailed the night before. She had stayed with Sheila at Mountain View B & B, which was closer to the trail. We planned to meet up by 9:00 to begin our hike.

Our first discovery in the kitchen was another woman and not Helen. This made us a little bit nervous. We ate our breakfast quickly, with Scott enjoying the traditional Full Irish and I had an omelet for a nice change. It was huge, maybe five eggs and full of cheese. I did my best, but I was to my breaking point and grossed out to be eating so many eggs every morning. Although I knew in the back of my mind it was good fuel for the hike ahead.

As we finished our meal we saw the time was 8:50, we asked the woman where we could find Helen. Shortly thereafter, Helen arrived and we loaded into her car. It was dreary, raining, and not the most wonderful start to our day.

We arrived to see Betsy standing on the side of the road waiting for us in the rain. Luckily she was in great spirits and wasn't concerned we were a little bit late. We waved goodbye to Helen and set off up the road. Up is the keyword as it seemed we always began our day with a big climb.

The first section we literally climbed a mountain. Why was I surprised?

The waymarkers led us up a paved road. By the time we reached the top, it was only lightly raining and warm. The views were pretty with rugged green mountain all around.

Scott and I enjoyed hiking with Betsy. We walked at the same pace and shared stories of our lives. The time seemed to pass quickly.

Eventually, we turned off the road and went over the first of many livestock ladders of the day. Up a mountain we went, it was mucky and wet. The views were pretty in every direction and there were always grazing sheep to watch. Near the top, we hiked in dense fog for a while. It was eerie how quiet it became. Next, we hiked downhill and it was tough going. The mud was the deepest we had seen yet on the Beara Way. It was hard mentally and physically as we tried to stay on our feet. We definitely could not have done it without trekking poles. Without them, it would have taken twice as long.

Suddenly, another couple joined us on our descent. They were a young German couple we met at our B & B a few nights back. We saw them off and on through our day. They didn't have trekking poles and we really didn't know how they were maneuvering the mountain. The young woman had terrible blisters on her toes, so I gave her some of my silicone toe tubes. Our feet were too wet for bandages to stay attached.

The countryside was lush and green. The rain finally stopped and we saw a lake in the valley far below. On the other side of the lake was a huge waterfall in the distance.

Eventually, we made it to the lake and walked on the roadway alongside it. The water reflected the sky and shimmered a gunmetal gray.

We met a man who dropped off his dog near us. The dog then proceeded to gather up all of the sheep we could see and chase them home. Down the road, they all went and the dog followed up behind. It was cool to see a farm dog in action and we were impressed with his herding skills.

After a while, we came to a pretty creek and stopped to eat our lunch. It was a feast of fruit, nuts, and sandwiches that Betsy brought along.

After lunch and plenty of water, we began another long uphill grade. It was followed by an exhausting downhill. They all began to look the same with thick grass, mud, and sheep. We were getting tired. It was such mental work to get through the mud safely.

Finally, we made it down the last mountain and to a paved road. We knew we were getting closer to the town of Kenmare. Here and there we saw homes and ranches. We became sentimental as it was our last day and last miles of the Beara Way.

Scott:

It felt good to know we had almost completed our goal of hiking the Beara Way. It was more challenging and muddier than we had imagined, but it felt like a good accomplishment.

My feet were aching so much and I was exhausted. I chanted to myself a mantra as I walked along quietly behind Scott and Betsy. It was something like this: "I am strong. I can do this. My feet are fine. My legs are strong." My mantra really did work. It's just mind over matter and not dwelling on the negative. It gave me a little bit more energy to finish out the hike.

The homes began getting closer together and soon we walked through entire neighborhoods. We enjoyed seeing the different homes and yards with landscaping and flowers.

After 7.5 hours and 16 miles of hiking, we walked into the picturesque town of Kenmare. Kenmare means "Head of the sea" because it sits at the head of Kenmare Bay.

Kenmare instantly reminded us of a town near our home in California called Nevada City. Both charming small towns set on a hillside.

Our hike on the Beara Way was complete!

The three of us stood on a corner at the entrance to the town. We tried to decide which direction to walk in order to find our pre-arranged lodgings. Betsy was to stay the night at a home owned by her host from the prior night, Sheila.

Just as we discussed this, who pulls up to the curb in her car next to us? Sheila! Betsy greeted her with a surprise and introduced us. Sheila said to me, "I know you. You're the Bingo winner!"

We all laughed. Our Bingo game a few nights before seemed like a lifetime ago to me.

Shelia drove us to her home just outside of town and we dropped Betsy off. We agreed to clean up and meet for a nice dinner later.

Shelia drove us to our B & B a short distance away. We sure appreciated her kindness because we were muddy and exhausted.

Our B & B was a normal looking house in a neighborhood just below the town. Scott and I were dead tired, soaking wet and hungry, which isn't the best way to arrive at a new place. We stood on the front porch, removed our wet socks, boots, and gators. Tom, an older gentleman answered our knock. He seemed surprised to see us as I explained Helen had recommended his place and I had booked a room through Expedia the night before.

He left us on the porch to go back inside to check his computer for our reservation. Once it was found he came back to invite us inside. He was a bit gruff and didn't seem very keen to have wet hikers arriving at his door. We were shown to our room and he gave us plastic bags to store our wet clothing. It wasn't the warm welcome we were used to, but we decided you never know what's going on in someone's life right at that moment.

After our hot showers, we went to the front room to enjoy a nice bit of Irish hospitality of tea and cookies. Sugar and hot tea make everything better.

Later, we met Betsy and walked into town. It was a priority for the three of us to find an ATM machine. With that chore complete we found the perfect restaurant for dinner. Davitt's Restaurant couldn't have been a better choice.

We sat by a warm fire with many people around, but it wasn't too crowded or noisy. What a treat! We enjoyed a nice red wine to start and then I ate my favorite vegetable soup so far in Ireland. That's saying a lot because I ate it in every town, every day. Scott ordered Jambalaya. Betsy had a huge bowl of clams and I scarfed down an order of prawns. It was an amazing meal and the perfect way to celebrate the end of our day.

We weren't finished though, the three of us popped into a pub for a final nightcap and to enjoy live music. It was traditional Irish music and we enjoyed the tunes.

Later, we said our final goodbye to Betsy. She was getting a ride the next morning to the Sheepshead Peninsula where she would begin her hike on the Sheep's Head Way. We were all happy and sad. Sad to part ways, but happy and excited to move on to a new adventure in Ireland.

For Scott and I, it meant a rest day and time to see the sights in Kenmare, followed by a day's hike on the Kerry Way into Killarney.

REST DAY IN KENMARE

Scott and I just finished our week-long hike of the Beara Way and enjoyed a nice day of rest in Kenmare. The town was a perfect place to recharge, with a laundromat and plenty of restaurants and accommodations.

Kenmare is a small town full of charm and history. Only a short walk from town center is the Kenmare Stone Circle, a fairy tree, and Cromwell's Bridge.

First thing in the morning, we checked out of our lodgings with the intent to stay at a hotel in the town center. I had checked online for availability and we were in luck, a perk to travel in the offseason.

We walked into town and went into the Coachman's Hotel. They were very kind and said there was a room available. We expected to have to return in the afternoon for check-in but they had a room ready right then! We were happy to stay in a nicer, large room. We unpacked our backpacks and gathered our dirty laundry. This day would be about getting some of our chores done; laundry and resupplying food for the trail. The laundry mat was nearby and we put a load in to wash. Then, I set my timer on my phone and we went to enjoy a cup of coffee at the bakery.

After we put our wet clothing into the dryer we went down the street to find Cromwell's Bridge. It was easy to find and we read about its history. The local lore believes the monks built the bridge in the 11th Century. The bridge has a very steep arch and is made of ancient rocks. Moss and greenery cover parts of it. It's a picturesque scene.

Just a few steps away we found the Fairy tree, which is tied with good wishes and prayers. Next to that, was the Kenmare Stone Circle. It was amazing to see these standing stones, 15 around the circle with one in the center. It is said they were set during the Bronze Age (2,200-500 B.C.).

We were quite productive during our laundry time and enjoyed exploring Kenmare.

Our afternoon was spent relaxing and we went to the same restaurant as the night before for a big dinner. We actually ate the same meals again because we were so happy with them.

Our plan for the next day was to hike over the mountains, through Killarney National Park, and into Killarney.

We went to bed early and loved the little splurge of a hotel room.

KERRY WAY

Kenmare to Killarney

Our plan was to hike from Kenmare over the mountains, through the Killarney National Park, and into the city of Killarney. This hike is stage nine on the Kerry Way. It is the most popular long-distance waymarked trail in Ireland, as well as the longest at 134 miles. Stage nine is rated moderate to strenuous in difficulty and is 16 miles long. We learned quickly as we hiked through Ireland not to bother starting out too early. It was unlikely we could get coffee before 8:00 a.m. in most small towns.

This day was no different, as we waited for the local French coffee shop, Maison Gourmet, to open at 8:00. We were the first customers of the day and enjoyed coffee and delicious, fresh croissants. After our small breakfast, we stopped at a market to buy apples and bananas for our hike. Slowly, we made our way out of town. The sky was grey and the temperature cool.

Soon, sweat dripped down our faces as we climbed out of town through the neighborhoods on Old Kenmare Road. Eventually, the road became dirt and we could see only mountains and no more homes. We walked along quietly as it began to drizzle rain. The views behind us of the Kenmare area displayed the beautiful, green farmland, as far as the eye could see.

Suddenly, a woman on horseback sped by followed by her black dog, who sprinted like the wind. Our hoods were up over our heads against the rain and we never even heard her approach. It began to rain harder and I wondered what in the heck we were doing? Who chooses to hike over mountains in the rain? At the top we didn't even stop to rest. The wind blew the rain in a slant at our faces. I was focused on keeping one foot in front of the other with my goal to get off the mountain.

We made our way between Peakeen and Knockanaguish Mountains and into the Windy Gap.

The descent was a special challenge as water streamed downhill, and turned the trail into a creek.

I have to mention the apple I snacked on as I walked. Almost every day we ate apples as we hiked. The apples in Ireland are by far the most delicious I have tasted anywhere in the world. They are sweet and tart at the same time and taste like candy!

After we descended the mountain, we unknowingly entered Killarney National Park. The uplands of the park were wide open plains surrounded by towering mountains.

We followed our waymarked trail. It was so peaceful and quiet with not a soul to be seen. Only a few native red deer were scattered across the hillsides.

Later, we turned onto another trail which took us up into a forest. Green moss covered every tree and rock. It was gorgeous. The rain had stopped and it was unbelievably peaceful. This is why we hike, I thought, as my rain gear slowly dried out.

In the forest I imagined fairies and trolls, it was the perfect place for my imagination to run wild.

A few minutes later we passed a couple hiking in the opposite direction. Then, another group of six teenagers and an adult passed. Civilization must be near we thought.

How wonderful to hike in a national park where they try to protect the land! We were beyond happy to see railroad ties and narrow boardwalks over the muddy bog areas of the trail. We may be wet, but not covered in mud!

Scott randomly found a credit card next to the trail and worried it must have been lost by a hiker. (Later in the day in Killarney, Scott turned it into the bank where they would call the owner right away.)

We stopped to take a break at the Cores Cascade, a small waterfall just off the trail. A perk of hiking in Ireland? Seeing waterfalls every day. It was a gradual descent for the rest of the afternoon, usually near the Owengarrif River.

At one point, we could see far below to the lakes of Killarney. Finally, we entered the section of Killarney National Park which was more populated near the Torc Waterfall. First, we descended many stairs which lead us to the magnificent falls. The Torc Waterfall is about 80 feet high and is truly beautiful. Unfortunately, our cell phones couldn't capture the size and beauty of the falls to do it justice. It was a pretty spot, popular with tourists and a must-see attraction in Killarney.

Eventually, we arrived at a road and parking lot. There were no waymarked arrows anywhere. We saw some jaunting cars and their drivers parked to one side. These are horse-drawn buggies the tourists may hire to explore the area. This was still the Killarney National Park and there were pathways all around the lakes.

One of the drivers gave us directions to the town of Killarney which was still a few miles away. Of course, the rain began to fall again and we were wet and tired. For a while, we walked the cement path next to the lake. We passed the historic Muckross House, a 19th Century mansion. It's a popular tourist attraction and quite a picturesque sight.

We became more and more tired when up ahead we saw more jaunting carts who waited for tourists. After we paid too much money (25 euros) we climbed into the buggy out of the rain and continued on our way. We enjoyed the stories our driver told us about the National Park, Muckross House, and the Abbey. He had grown up in the area and was a wealth of knowledge.

Later, he dropped us off at the main road into Killarney and we only had another mile or so to walk to our hotel. I was sure glad we had booked a room the night before, so we didn't need to roam around town in search of a room.

After seven hours and 16 miles, we arrived in Killarney. It had been a day of highs and lows with the rain and wet trails. The beauty of the national park was stunning. We were so pleased we decided to hike the Kerry Way, even if for only a day.

BIKE AROUND KILLARNEY

Killarney proved to be a town full of culture and entertainment. It is located in South Western Ireland, with plenty of outdoor activities to keep visitors entertained. We spent several days there for our conference and took time in between activities to explore the area.

For only 15 euros each, Scott and I were able to rent bicycles. We were given brief instructions on how to brake and shift gears. Then, we were given a map of the area. Since we hiked through Killarney National Park and into town, we had an idea of where we would like to explore.

The first place on our list was the Ross Castle. It was about a fifteen-minute bike ride from our hotel. I was nervous about riding on the roads for part of the way, but it wasn't bad. We just needed to be extra cautious of the cars, as they drove on the opposite side of the road than we are used to back in California.

The Ross Castle was before us on the shore of Lower Killarney Lake called Lough Leane. It was built in the 15th century by one of the O'Donoghue Ross chieftains. We parked our bikes and walked around the castle property. It was especially picturesque next to the lake.

Next, we hopped on our bikes to explore the 150 acres of property and trails behind the castle. I was surprised by the trail system and how much fun we had on our ride there. Our first stop on the trail was the old copper mine. It was in use until the early 1900's . The section we saw was now flooded with lake water. After we were on our bikes again, several minutes later we made a stop at Governor's Rock. It's a lookout point over the lake which gives a beautiful lake view in each direction.

After we explored the island, we rode through part of town. With many different restaurants and pubs, you could easily spend all day downtown. It was too busy for us, so we got on the bike path back and rode into Killarney National Park. The path meanders along the side of the lake and led us to our next stop.

From the path, we could see the lake and the other direction we could see the Muck Ross Friary. After we parked our bikes we explored the grounds of the Friar's Abbey, which was founded in the 1400's by Donal MacCarthy. There were many tombstones in the yard and we stopped to read them and wondered about their stories. I would say 80% of the women's names were Margaret, which we found of interest as we looked at the stones. The friary was in excellent condition. We wandered the rooms and admired the detailed cement work and window shapes.

The wind began to chill us to the bone and it slowly became colder, so we made our way back to the bike shop. We enjoyed our time on the bike immensely and it was a highlight of our visit to Killarney.

TIME TO LEAVE KILLARNEY

It was our final morning in Killarney. The night before was the closing party for our travel blogging conference. We stayed out too late, drank wine and danced and generally enjoyed ourselves at a pub.

We moved slowly as we checked out of the hotel, but we were on a mission before our next hike. We wanted to play golf in Ireland!

Our hotel clerk had reserved us a tee-time for 9:00 a.m. to play nine holes of golf at a nearby course. A taxi picked us up and delivered us to the course on time. When we tried to go into the clubhouse to check in, it was locked up and closed. There wasn't a person to be seen.

We were bundled up against the cold and a little bit hung over. Finally, a woman pulled up and got out of her car. She asked, "Do you have a tee-time today?"

We said, "Yes, it was at 9:00."

"Great," she exclaimed as she proceeded to get us set up with golf clubs and general information for the course. She was friendly and didn't mention our later start time.

At first, we struggled. It was a bitter wind and we played with clubs which were unfamiliar. Eventually, we warmed up and got into the game. By the end, we had enjoyed a fine time.

Scott:

I was so excited as I prepared to hit my first tee shot in Ireland. I took a few practice swings and lined myself up. The excitement faded as I watched my first shot slice out of bounds. Just like home. We did enjoy our game very much, after all, how often do you get to play golf in Ireland?

After our game, we took a taxi to the bus station. Our next destination was the Dingle Peninsula. We planned to hike a couple of days on the Dingle Way. The start of our hike would be the town of Dingle.

First, we took a public bus to Tralee which was about 40 km away from Killarney. After a short wait, we rode on another bus 50 km to Dingle.

Dingle sits at the tip of the peninsula and is a popular destination for fishing and tourism in general. It is well known that Fungie the Bottlenosed Dolphin has been a big attraction in the bay since 1983.

After we arrived in Dingle and checked in to our bed & breakfast, we enjoyed a delicious dinner of pizza and garlic bread at a nearby Italian restaurant. This was a wonderful change from the standard pub fare, and probably the first day we didn't eat soup since we had arrived in Ireland!

EXPLORATION DAY IN DINGLE

D ingle has so much to offer, we decided to spend a day there to discover its wonders. It was wonderful to enjoy a light breakfast of pastries with coffee instead of our heavier breakfast with eggs. Our plan was to explore the area early before the predicted rain arrived in the afternoon.

First, we found the Visitor's Center. An enthusiastic woman listened to our plans to hike the next two-days on the Dingle Way. She explained that we should make reservations for lodging right then. Now that it was October many places had closed for the season. For our first night, after a fifteen-mile hike, we would stay in a hostel. She let us know we needed to bring our own food as there wouldn't be any at the hostel and since it wasn't near a town, there were no pubs as an option.

She also made us a reservation at a bed & breakfast in a village which was fifteen miles beyond our first night's lodgings. The helpful woman shared her ideas of fun things to do around Dingle for the day.

First, we strolled around the marina to examine the boats and watch the birds which congregated on them.

Then, we found the trail which ran along the beach. This trail led us to the lighthouse at the point. We enjoyed our walk along the bay and being near the ocean. It was cloudy but comfortable outside. We were happy to see cows graze along the trail. Ahead were the remnants of the Eask Tower, built in 1847. The tower was 40 feet tall and there to alert sailors to let down their sails as they safely entered Dingle Harbor.

Just past the tower, we spotted Slaidin Beach. It's a popular spot to see sea life. We combed the shore for shells and watched the birds search for their next meal. We didn't actually see any sea life but it was okay.

Eventually, we made our way to the lighthouse. In 1887 it was completed at the mouth of Dingle Harbor. It offered pleasing views, and we paused to watch the fishing boats pass by. It began to sprinkle rain as we made our way back to town. We ate our leftover pizza from the previous night, which Scott carried in his daypack.

Because the rain began in full force, Scott suggested it was time to get indoors and visit the Dingle Oceanworld Aquarium. It didn't really interest me, as I don't usually care to see animals in captivity. Scott pointed out how the aquarium houses animals which have been injured or rescued. They strive to breed species which are depleting in numbers. He convinced me, so off we went.

We arrived just in time to see the otters being fed. There was so much joy as they ran around with fish heads in their mouths, chasing each other. They played and played while we laughed and laughed. The small children near us who watched the otter's hijinks squealed with delight and excitement. After we watched the otter we spent some time at the different fish tanks.

The seahorses intrigued me most. I learned that the male seahorse carries the babies and gives birth to up to 400 at a time. The seahorses have armored plates instead of scales and are slow swimmers. Luckily, they can change colors to hide from predators! Another one of our favorites were the starfish. We didn't know they eat meat and love clams, oysters, fish, and other small sea creatures.

Next, it was time for the penguins to be fed. The Gentoo are the third largest penguin species in the world and the fastest swimming bird in the world. We can vouch for that, as they fly through the water at surprising speeds.

When the handler came out to feed the penguins small fish, we laughed so hard at their antics. They flew out of the water like a bullet, jumping onto the ledge of ice to be fed. We were highly entertained. The aquarium has a snow machine and they make snow each day so the penguins can play.

If you decide to visit the Dingle Oceanworld Aquarium, be sure to look at their website for feeding times. They also list each of the penguin names and special characteristics; like which penguin they are paired up with, which are mates and what their habits are. Then, you can match the penguin to its color-coded band, so you know which one is which.

The aquarium has many other species and creatures big and small. Everywhere we turned, we saw turtles, sharks, bearded dragons, snakes and more! We were impressed with the conservation efforts taken by the aquarium. They have a lobster hatchery and practice lobster conservation and protection.

The aquarium also tags and releases Angel Sharks, and the day we visited they released a Loggerhead Turtle back into the sea after its successful rehabilitation.

We spent a lovely time on our rainy afternoon at the aquarium. Scott and I highly recommend a visit if you are in Dingle. Be sure to check out their website first for current pricing and discounts as well as times of the year they are closed for maintenance.

After the aquarium visit, we decided to look into a brewery tour we had seen advertised. Unfortunately, the tour was too pricey for our budget, but we were told to go into the bar and find some of the same beer.

We walked into Dick Mack's Pub, built in 1850 with whiskey bottles floor to ceiling on one wall. A "Snug" bookended each side of the bar which I found so charming. A snug is basically an enclosed, private seating area with access to the bar. In the center of the room was a long bar, maybe 15 feet long. Scott and I sat at barstools along the center bar and made ourselves comfortable with beer and a glass of wine. A few minutes later a woman walked into the pub and came right up to me.

"Are you selling belts?" she asked.

The question caught me off guard and I laughed, shaking my head "no."

She explained how the pub was originally a haberdashery where patrons came in to have a hat or belt custom made. The bar we sat at was an old workstation and even had an iron section for the hand leather work.

In old days, when customers came into the haberdashery, the owner told them to have a seat and enjoy a pint of beer while they waited. Customers weren't allowed to be charged for the beer because it wasn't a pub. Eventually, the haberdashery became a very popular pub instead, although to this day it is still considered a leather shop as well.

Soon, the bar filled with people. A group of six men from Dublin sat next to us at the bar. Much to our surprise, they began to sing Irish Folk songs. Two that I remember hearing were Molly Malone and Darby O'Leary. Scott and I enjoyed the music so much that we sat for hours and drank wine and beer. I even drank a half pint of Dick Mack's Coffee Stout! This was the first time in 27 years Scott and I drank beer together!

Later, we noticed the day getting away from us, so we went back to our B & B to wash laundry. We also needed to go out for a good dinner to absorb all of the alcohol we consumed.

Our rest day in Dingle didn't really involve rest, but we had a blast and it was one of our favorite days in Ireland.

DINGLE WAY DAY 1

Dingle to Dunquin

The Dingle Way runs 110 miles along the Dingle Peninsula. We planned to hike two days on it and maybe a third, depending on the weather. If we went onto the third day we were advised to skip that section of the hike due to the severe mud on the mountain. We didn't need to be told twice, as we had seen our share of mud on the Beara Way.

Our normal hiking routine back home began early in the morning. In Ireland, the lodgings are not necessarily available until later in the day, so it made for a different routine for us. The hostel we booked for our first day on the Dingle Way didn't allow entry until 5:00 p.m. We slept in until 8:00 a.m. and then devoured a greasy breakfast of eggs and ham on our way out of town.

Our hike began at 10:00 a.m. and was predicted to take about six to seven hours. For a while, the walk took us along Dingle Bay on pavement. Views of the bay and surrounding hillside kept us entertained. The weather felt perfect, no clouds, wind or rain. The hills shined green in the sunshine. This is what we came to Ireland to experience.

After some time we came to the Dingle Way waymarker which pointed straight up a hill. It was a narrow path between farms upon which cattle and sheep were transferred between pastures. I can't begin to tell you how much of a challenge this section was. The entire path consisted of mud and manure. It was deep, slippery, and slow going. Thank goodness (once again) for our trekking poles. Otherwise, we certainly would have been falling in the mud. By the time we reached the top, I felt beyond grouchy. The views of the ocean were nice and we saw a few horses, but by the time we hiked down the other side and returned to the paved road, I was mad.

If we had stayed on the paved road in the first place, it would have taken us ten minutes to get around the bend. The waymarkers directing us over the hill on livestock paths felt completely unnecessary, a waste of our time and energy.

A big discussion ensued as Scott and I discussed staying on the roadway vs. any trail detours we may encounter. We agreed Slea Head Road toward Dunquin was the best option. Plus, there were archeological sites we wanted to visit if we stuck to the roadway as well.

Our first site of interest was a ring fort or fairy fort as they are otherwise called. It was a round shaped, grassy area, surrounded by a circular mound at the edge and thick shrubs as a protective barrier. The ring forts are plentiful in Ireland, over 40,000 can be found. This happened to be our first and we were excited to learn about these homesteads which dated back to the Iron Age. The round shape of the fort allowed the clan and their cattle to be protected. Over time, the forts have become associated with fairies. For our family, they have special meaning as well. We named our first daughter "Shae" which means "From the fairie fort."

To visit the fort it cost a few euros for entry to the property. There were sheep and a horse nearby, so we bought grain snacks to feed them. The cute sheep waited patiently for a handout, but the horse (which stood very tall) pushed in front of the sheep and aggressively tried to get the food from Scott. Then, the horse got his hoof caught in the wire fence and I freaked out thinking he would end up injured. Luckily, before I could run for help, it became untangled.

After we explored the property, we hit the road again. It was amazing to walk above the ocean in the sunshine only wearing our short sleeves.

After a while, we came upon a pub. We enjoyed coffee as we sat on the patio and took in the gorgeous views of the Wild Atlantic Ocean. Some people, who we had previously seen at the fort pulled up in their car. The rest of the day we played piggyback, as we walked the narrow one-lane road and cars drove by, stopping at the same historic spots or car parks with a view.

The next historic stop we came upon was a place we had looked forward to seeing, the Bee Hive Huts. The huts are round structures built in clusters from rock and span a section of hillside. They are from the 12th Century and mortar wasn't used in the construction. Originally, many of the huts included straw roofs while others only rock.

We ran into a few people who were driving the Dingle Peninsula. At each stop, we had seen each other, even though they drove and we walked. This shows how slow going the roads are, being narrow and almost one lane.

On and on we walked through the afternoon. The views amazed us, only the pavement killed our feet. We stopped often to take pictures and take in the dramatic scenery.

After seven hours, exhausted but happy, we arrived at our hostel, Oige Youth Hostel. It was 5:00 p.m. sharp! Perfect timing. Our feet ached, so we removed our boots and relaxed outside on the patio for a while. The hostel sat above the Atlantic Ocean on the side of a hill. It had the picture-perfect location.

We cleaned up and settled into our room. It had several bunk beds, but only Scott and I were guests. Another perk to our hike at the end of the season was not sharing a room and having another ocean view room!

Dinner involved us heating up water for our soup pouches, which hit the spot. We enjoyed our meal on the patio before it became too cold. It was extra special to end our day with a sunset, rare as they were.

Sleep came early that night as we had walked 16 miles in seven hours. We were off to a good start on the Dingle Way.

DINGLE WAY DAY 2

Dunquin to Feohanagh/ Ballydavid

Scott and I woke up bright and early the next morning. The next section of the Dingle Way was 15 miles long and we predicted it would take five to seven hours to hike. The hostel was quiet, and it was a nice change to skip the big breakfast. We enjoyed fruit and cheese as we walked along.

The weather didn't cooperate and the rain came down in a drizzle as the fog surrounded us. To begin the day in bad weather was tough compared to the brilliant sunshine of the previous day.

I felt frustrated with the low visibility. We knew there were amazing ocean views around us, as well as mountain views of Mt. Brandon and Sybil Point.

Our destination was Feohanagh, where the woman from the Dingle Visitor Center had kindly booked our reservation at a B & B for the night.

We hiked for a couple hours on paved roads. It was not our idea of hiking at all. The Dingle Way trail system was a disappointment so far. Mainly, it was pavement walking with a few offshoots of muddy livestock trails. We were not impressed.

Finally, we came to a section of beach walking. The weather was calm, the water still and everything was gray but exceptionally picturesque. We took some of our favorite pictures in Ireland right there along the beach. The sky, ocean, and water on the beach all blended together to make us look as if we walked on water.

Butter Harbor is well known for its history in the butter trade and dates back to the time of Vikings. After five miles of hiking on the beach in wet sand, we were ready for coffee and a proper meal.

First, we discussed taking a side trip to the Gallarus Oratory. It's a famous church in the area that was built in the 12th Century, but we weren't motivated to go off the trail.

After the beach, we were back on pavement. The ocean was on our left with pastures of sheep between the water and the road. On our right were beautiful homes. Scott stopped to take photo #1000 of the Irish Sheep while I admired the homes in the neighborhood. What a picturesque place to live!

Soon, we arrived in the tiny village of Ballydavid. It's a big fishing port and we passed by a huge boat ramp. Scott noticed a restaurant and nearby hostel. Perfect timing, because we were hungry and cold.

We settled into the pub and I enjoyed a delicious potato and leek soup, while Scott tried their seafood chowder. This chowder was much different than any he had enjoyed in Ireland thus far. It had a clear broth with squid and a huge shrimp across the top of the bowl. Coffee sure hit the spot and we relaxed after our meal.

Scott brought out our Dingle Way map and the information for the Bed & Breakfast we were headed for. It looked to be an hour and a half walk to get to Feohanagh.

As we looked more closely at our B & B information, we realized it wasn't actually in the village of Feohanagh, but in the village of Ballydavid which is where we just enjoyed our lunch!

I looked at the picture of the B & B and said: "I think we already passed this place, it looks familiar."

We knew lodgings were limited this late in the season so we needed to make a decision. Do we go on to the next village and risk not being able to find a place to stay, or cut our day short after only four hours hike to stay at the pre-arranged B & B?

I voted that we stay as the rain came down again and my feet ached.

Scott was not thrilled with "our" decision but he agreed.

We asked the bartender where we could find our B & B and he said: "Oh, it's right back down the road, two minutes, next to the post office."

We laughed, thanked him and made sure to let him know we planned to return for dinner later.

Scott and I were so glad we stopped in Ballydavid for lunch. We would have been upset to miss out on our lodgings.

Back down the road we went, and there we spotted our cute B & B next to the post office. It was right in front of the sheep Scott had taken pictures of earlier. We were going to stay in one of the lovely homes I had admired!

Our sweet host allowed us to check in, even though it was before 3:00 p.m. We adored our room with the sheep (and ocean) view. After we cleaned up Scott and I sat in the sunroom which consisted entirely of windows. Our host brought out freshly made apple cobbler and hot tea. We relaxed for a while until another couple came in. They were from the U.S and had walked part of the Dingle Way as well. We chatted about our hiking experiences and future plans. It was nice to visit with someone on a similar path.

Once the rain stopped, Scott and I took a hike out of town to the cliffs I had read about. The ground was boggy like a sponge, but it was worth it. The cliffs were very dramatic and I imagined they were like small Cliffs of Moher. We stood for a while and listened to the waves of the Atlantic crash far below.

Later, we went back to the restaurant for dinner. The other couple we met earlier was there as well. We sat together for a few hours, drinking wine and exchanging stories of our lives. It was nice to spend time with others as we had been alone for some time.

Dinner filled our bellies with fish and chips. It tasted fabulous and not a bit greasy. We sure were impressed by the seafood from this area.

We turned in early with full stomachs and rested feet.

In the morning, after a huge breakfast of omelets, our host directed the four of us to the post office next door where we could catch the bus. Our new friends were headed home, and we were finished with our section of the Dingle Way and ready to move on.

Our next destination was Doolin, further north on the West Coast. But first, we had four busses and seven hours of travel ahead of us.

The busses were comfortable and we encountered no problems as we changed buses at the different stations. The longest we waited in between transfers was 15 minutes. Public transportation in Ireland is easy and convenient.

DOOLIN

cott and I sat on the bus as it made its way toward the west coast of Ireland, more specifically the village of Doolin. This area is known for the Cliffs of Moher. We had WIFI on the bus, so I looked online at hikes in the area. The Doolin Cliff Hike to the Cliffs of Moher was mentioned and we decided it would be the perfect hike for us.

Eventually, after walking all around Doolin for 30 minutes, we found a bed & breakfast with a room available for the night. I asked our host about the hike to the Cliffs of Moher. She made a quick phone call and let us know there was a three-hour guided tour at 10:00 am the next morning, from Doolin to the Cliffs of Moher. Scott and I discussed taking a guided hike vs. just figuring it out on our own. In hindsight, we are so glad to have chosen to be guided, and we know we supported an amazing cause.

At 10:00 a.m. sharp, Scott and I, as well as 15 other people met in front of O'Connor's Pub. Pat Sweeney talked to us about the trail and the history behind it.

In 2006, there was economic struggle in the area and the farmers looked for different ways to bring tourists to Doolin. The solution was to create a trail system. Pat, as well as 39 other farmers, allowed hikers to pass through their land, making the trail accessible through all of the different farm properties. Now tourists visit Doolin specifically to hike and when the trail system is complete, it will be 20k long. Pat left us with two guides, Charlie and Beth. Our group set off to hike the three hour, 8km section which is now complete. The fee was a 10-euro donation at the end of the hike, to help support more work on the trail, as well as maintenance of the existing section.

According to the guide maps, the Burren Way is a 123 km route which includes the coast of Doolin to the Cliffs of Moher.

Our hike began in the main village of Doolin and took us along the cliffs which overlooked the ocean. It began as a sunny morning and the trail was between rolling green hills of farmland and the wild, Atlantic Ocean. We saw a few cows and even a castle off in the distance! Charlie and Beth kept a fast pace for us and told stories when we stopped for a moment. The scenery was magnificent and we took many pictures along the way.

Every step and every direction we enjoyed the most gorgeous views. As we looked back, we could see Doolin in the distance. Far out in the ocean, we could see the Arayan Islands. The trail turned to single track along the cliff's edge. I felt a bit anxious to be so near the edge, especially with the powerful winds. The ocean was so rough that the boats weren't even going out to the islands.

The group we hiked with was very diverse with people from around the world. A few of us were equipped with hiking boots, trekking poles, and were mentally prepared for the mud from the trail which would be ahead. Scott and I had hiked in Ireland for weeks, so we knew the wet, muddy bog situation, which was sure to come.

Some people in our group wore denim jeans, sweatshirts, and regular tennis shoes and were still able to hike just fine. After an hour it began to rain. It had been perfectly sunny and then the clouds rolled in. The weather in Ireland constantly changed and it was best to be prepared for anything. Luckily, Scott and I were already in our rain jackets. They were lightweight and kept us dry.

Charlie stopped the group and explained how we would see a reverse waterfall, a few minutes up the trail.

The water fell dramatically into the ocean but the wind picked it back up and threw it onto the trail. It headed straight at us! If we weren't soaked by the rain then, we sure were after that! What a crazy experience, as I have never seen a waterfall blowback before.

In the second hour of the hike, it rained off and on. The trail was wet with many creek crossings. I was thankful for my trekking poles, which helped me balance in the wind and were like a third foot going over creeks. We hiked a section of muddy bog farmland and one person even fell. Her entire backside was covered in mud. I remember those days of falling in the mud as we hiked the Beara Way. It was not very fun. Still, we felt lucky the farmer allowed us to cross his land.

During our last hour, the sun began to shine. We were thankful to dry out a bit, but there were still areas where the ocean sprayed us with water. We joked about how we were getting the "Irish Baptism."

At one point as we had paused to take pictures and chat with the other hikers, we noticed one of the couples off to the side near the edge of the cliff. The man went down on his knee and proposed to his girlfriend. We all clapped and cheered after she said yes. What a special memory they will always cherish.

Slowly, we made our way higher and higher. Charlie and Beth let us know where it was safe or unsafe to take pictures from. Scott liked to get a bit too close to the edge for my taste, so I stayed by myself, far back from the cliff's edge. Eight people had died in 2017 so far from falls off the cliffs (some suicides) and we didn't want to be added to those statistics.

After our last climb, we arrived at the highest point of our hike, 700 feet above the churning sea. Right in front of us stood the world-famous Cliffs of Moher. They were beautiful and dramatic with the Atlantic Ocean below.

We spent time in the tourist area atop the cliffs. There were plenty of pictures to be taken, although it was a huge challenge in the strong winds. I could see how someone might easily be blown off the cliffs.

At the prearranged time, we met our guides and boarded a bus which returned us to the village of Doolin. Scott and I absolutely enjoyed our Doolin Cliff hike. For me, it may have been one of my favorite experiences in Ireland.

Everyone in our group enjoyed themselves, even the people who were not dressed properly for the elements. I would definitely recommend hiking boots and a rain jacket, just so you will be able to focus on the beauty of the area and not being wet.

We highly recommend this hike. There is so much hard work which goes into the trail maintenance, as well as the expansion of the rest of the distance. We hope other people will hike it as a group, make some new friends and contribute to their trail project.

THE IN-BETWEEN

We enjoyed our short time in Doolin and only spent two nights. Ireland is such a big country and we had more to explore. We spent a few days in Galway, including a day trip by tour bus to Connemara National Park and the Kylemore Abbey, which is stunning.

Eventually, we made our way east by train to Dublin. The train ride was our first in Ireland. The ride felt smooth, fast and the perfect way to see the country quickly.

Scott and I ended up at a boutique hotel in the Temple Bar district of Dublin. All I can say is the city is crazy and busy with so much happening all of the time. We did the typical tourist things; walk across Ha'penny Bridge, which is a symbol of the city, pass by the statue of Molly Malone, and Dublin Castle, which dates back to 1204.

The Temple Bar District is a hub of pubs, boutique shops, and music. It's also very loud, with dancing in the streets at night.

We didn't stay long, as we were headed on a new "Way" in Eastern Ireland, the Wicklow Way!

WICKLOW WAY DAY 1

Scott and I spent a restless night at our hotel (Blooms), even though it was a perfect location. All through the night, it sounded like the biggest party in the streets, even with my earplugs in. We awoke to our bathroom flooded with water, so our morning began very slowly.

After we checked out of Blooms we went to a small grocery store up the street to buy snacks and fruit for our hike. The hotel staff was so helpful and friendly. They advised us to take the #16 bus which would take us to the suburbs of Dublin. Our destination was Marlay Park, about 30 minutes away by bus in the suburb of Rathfarnham.

We found the correct bus and explained to the driver where we wanted to stop. He told us to just stay on the bus and he would let us know when it was time to get off, probably 30 minutes or so into the route.

Marlay Park was the start point of the 131 km (81 miles) Wicklow Way. This was one of the 40+ waymarked trails in Ireland, as well as the first official "Way", which began in 1982. The trail crosses the Wicklow Mountains and is supposed to be dryer and less boggy than some of the other hikes.

There is a special feeling of anticipation as we begin any long hike, and this was no different.

We didn't have a serious plan set in stone, only that we had a few days to hike before we ended our month-long stay in Ireland.

At first, we had been concerned because Hurricane Ophelia was making her way toward Ireland, but no one in Dublin had seemed concerned. So, we pressed on with our plan.

At Marley Park, we walked around for a while and looked for way markers. The park is huge! It's very green with lots of trees and paths going off in every direction. We saw many visitors out for a jog or even families spending time together.

Finally, we found the start point of the Wicklow Way! It's a monument and sign, so I took a picture of Scott with the monument before we began our hike. Little did I know, the mountains in the picture behind him we would hike over shortly.

Scott and I followed the way markers through the park, which was actually a challenge. We needed to ask for assistance from people several times to be sure we walked in the right direction.

At the edge of the park are restrooms, which was perfect timing, before we got on the road for a while.

Uphill we went, first on pavement, then dirt road. We met a couple who lived nearby and were out for their morning walk. They previously walked the Camino de Santiago in Spain, so we had some things in common. The conversation was fun as we hiked all the way up the mountain. They told us most people take 5-7 days to hike the Wicklow Way and end in Clonegal.

Near the top, we stopped to enjoy the sprawling city views of Dublin. The couple turned off onto a different trail and we proceeded up the mountain. There were many day hikers and runners on the trail. We were excited to hike on a nice, dry trail like we were used to back home. By the time we reached the top of Kilmashogue Mountain, I needed a break. We took time for a snack and a few moments to admire the views.

One of the main differences we noticed as we hiked along were all of the trees. There were Sitka Spruce, Scots Pine, and Beech. The other trails along the Beara and Dingle had fewer trees.

The weather remained comfortable and we walked along at a nice pace. How thrilled we were to walk in dry boots!

Later, we did some road walking and hill climbing, but nothing too steep. At one point, we hiked down a very wooded and secluded trail. The trees were so dense and it was quite dark. Scott spotted an Amanita, which is a gorgeous red mushroom, the kind fairies live near. I love when we find a cool mushroom, not to eat, only to admire. Especially these, as they are known to be poisonous.

Soon, we encountered writing on the pavement with an arrow which directed us to the Knockree Youth Hostel. It's only a few minutes off the Wicklow Way.

We checked in and went to our room. What a wonderful room we ended up with! It felt spacious and windows covered one entire wall, floor to ceiling. A bonus was that we had our own bathroom. The hostel sits on the side of a hillside so we could see far into the valley below. Sugarloaf Mountain and Maulin Mountain were in the distance and we watched herds of sheep grazing. What a treat, as it was certainly one of our best views of the trip.

After our hike, we happened to be quite wiped out. A twelve-mile hike after little sleep the previous night left us exhausted. Instead of cooking a meal in the hostel kitchen, we devoured our leftover snacks and an entire bag of black licorice we had bought as a souvenir for my Dad. Sorry, Dad!

The staff at the hostel expressed concern about the impending hurricane. The sky became cloudy and the wind began to blow harder. We spent some time online tracking Hurricane Ophelia's path and touched base with our family back home.

It was time to make a plan for the next day, but we decided to sleep on it and see what the morning would bring.

EPILOGUE

The morning brought more hurricane worries. And this is where the three options came in:

Option #1
Hunker down at the youth hostel on the hillside and wait out Hurricane Ophelia. The risks being huge glass windows which could turn into lethal weapons, probable lack of electricity, and little food to choose from in the hostel pantry.

Option #2
Get on the road and hike several miles to the nearest village and hope to find an available accommodation to wait out the hurricane.

Option #3
Get back on Ireland's famous Wicklow Way Trail and put in as many miles as possible before finding a town to spend the night.

The hostel provided a huge breakfast which was included in our price, a rare thing at hostels. The staff advised us to stay off the trail and spend another night at the hostel, (it wasn't fully booked) or walk the 7.5 km on the road into the small village of Enniskerry. After much thought and consideration, we said thank you and goodbye and hit the pavement. We decided to try our luck at a bed & breakfast in town, hopefully with a pub nearby.

The wind picked up and the trees swayed back and forth as we walked downhill toward town. The weather felt ominous and we hustled to get to a safe place before the storm arrived. We found it hard to believe the bus system had shut down in preparation for the hurricane. The streets were silent except for the little tap of our hiking poles as we walked along.

As soon as we walked into the picturesque village of Enniskerry, I saw the cutest B & B ever. The building was two stories tall and all white with red trim. A front garden complemented the yard. As we walked up to the entry gate I said, "We are staying there, I don't care how much the cost!"

Lucky for us they had an available room and our host allowed us to check in early, due to the impending hurricane. The price was reasonable and we were ecstatic to have a nice place to wait out the storm.

Our host gave us the weather reports and explained how rare it was to have a hurricane hit Ireland. The last hurricane to hit was in 1961. Ophelia seemed to be on a south to north track, and because things were still quiet, he suggested we walk up the street and visit the most beautiful gardens in Ireland at the world famous Powerscourt Estate.

We quickly bundled up and walked up the hill to the edge of town. The entrance gate to the Powerscourt property was closed due to the impending hurricane. Everyone was making their way home to batten down the hatches.

We saw a sign for the Powerscourt Waterfall and stood on the corner to discuss how far away it may be. After a moment, a woman drove by, she stopped her car and explained to us that it was too far to walk and that it was probably closed due to the weather. We thanked her and moved along.

Later, we ended up back in town at a pub where we sipped wine and filled our stomachs with hot vegetable soup. Our decision was made to return to the gardens after the storm had passed in the morning.

The hurricane blew through all evening and into the night. The wind gusts were huge and a bit frightening, but luckily the town didn't lose power. We sat in our room and watched the trees blow in the wind. The night was uncertain and nerve-wracking. Scott and I had never been in a hurricane before and didn't know what to expect.

THE AFTERMATH

Our host told us stories of the hurricane from the news. It had sustained winds of 119 miles per hour and was the most powerful hurricane ever recorded in the Eastern Atlantic. Three people tragically lost their lives in the storm which swept across the country.

Amazingly, as if nothing had ever happened, the sun shined bright and early the next morning. Everything was crisp and clear. Every leaf was blown from the trees, but the nearby property seemed in good shape.

Scott and I decided to try another visit to the gardens before we boarded a bus to the Wicklow Mountains National Park.

Out of town, we walked and up to the gates of the estate, which, fortunately, were open this time.

The main road through the property was littered with tree branches, as we saw several fallen trees along the way.

The golf course looked to be in good shape from our perspective so we walked on toward the house and gardens.

The Powerscourt House is stunning and considered one of the top mansions in the world via Lonely Planet. It is home to a variety of boutiques which sell local art, jewelry, and food.

This is where we bought our entry tickets for the garden and were given headphones for the audio tour.

We spent some time and walked the property. Luckily in the main gardens they only lost one huge tree to the storm. Workers already removed the limbs and were cleaning up the property.

The Powerscourt Estate history is so interesting and the gardens are gorgeous. It's a definite must see if you are near Dublin. And a fun fact to go with that is, Enniskerry is only 15 miles south of Dublin by car, which is hard for us to comprehend after hiking all day and spending the night in the foothills of the Wicklow Mountains. It feels like a different world, compared to the city.

Scott:

Before we end our story, there is one more hike we want to share with you. Even though it isn't technically one of the waymarked trails of Ireland, it is a trail system worth checking out.

After we left the Powerscourt Estate we took a bus to Wicklow Mountains National Park. Somehow, we were sidetracked off of the Wicklow Way and decided to hike in the National Park instead. We only had two days left and wanted to end our trip with a great hike.

After we got off the bus at the National Park, we got a room at the Glendalough Hotel which sits on the property. It was more money than we had been spending for lodgings but there really weren't many options.

We spent some time at the visitor center and visited the Monastic Site and graveyard.

There was a large map of the park's trail system so Jaynie and I went over the routes and planned which one would be best to take the next morning. Today the trails were closed due to the hurricane and they were assessing damage. We were only able to go for a short hike, but it gave us a feel for what was ahead.

We choose the Spinc and Glenealo Valley Hike. Spinc means pointed hill which gave us an idea of what to expect on our hike. It was a 9k loop with a suggested hike time of three hours. The trail was rated moderate with some elevation changes and included 600 wooden stairs.

Our hotel was situated right near the trail system. The clerk at the hotel suggested we hike the Spinc and Glenealo Valley Hike in reverse, counterclockwise, to get the most impressive views. We began our hike from the hotel (the only one) right next to the visitor center and Monastic Site. Each trail has a different colored arrow to follow and we followed the white arrow route. It is one of the nine waymarked trails in the park.

First, Scott and I followed the road and then got onto the trail which is just to the right of the lower lake.

After the lower lake, we came to the upper lake and it was so picturesque. The water was calm and the autumn colors from the trees reflected in the water. Between the lower and upper lakes was an information office and the start of many trails.

At this point, we needed to decide to follow the white arrows up the mountain to the left of the lake and hike clockwise, or stay to the right. We choose to take the clerk's advice and went right.

The trails followed along the right side of the upper lake, just above lake level.

Eventually, we arrived at the Glenealo Valley where a stream flowed into the upper lake. There wasn't a person around, only the red deer which live in the valley. It was October and the Red Stag rut season. Their calls echoed hauntingly through the entire valley.

At the start of our climb, we passed through the remains of an old mining camp. Lead was mined in the area in previous times. Uphill we climbed next to a fast flowing stream which cascaded into small waterfalls every few minutes. Sometimes, we stopped to take a break from the many switchbacks and watched the water falling down the mountain. We also looked back into the valley to see how far we had come. The views of the lakes were beautiful. Eventually, we climbed all the way up the gap in the mountains and only saw a few people along the way.

At the top, the trail turned to the left and then climbed up and up to scale the ridgeline. At this point, we began to see people who hiked from the opposite direction. Hiking the Wicklow Mountains National Park trail was such a treat, instead of soggy feet from the wet, muddy bog, there were narrow wooden boardwalks for us to walk on. There were park employees hard at work replacing sections of the wooden walkway. We wondered how on earth they got those wooden beams up to the top of the mountain ridge. One of the workers said the wood was flown in by helicopter. It must be a never-ending job to replace the wood because there is so much moisture every day and so many people who walk that section. It is good job security and you only need to hike up and down a mountain every day to get to work! Eventually, we began to pass other hikers who were hiking the route in the opposite direction than we were. Their back was to the lakes far below and we had the full view in front of us. The clerk was right and we were glad we took her advice.

Later, we stopped to eat our apples and take pictures. It was time to begin our descent. The hike down, step by step was slow going. The 600 wooden steps were narrow and now there were so many people coming from the other direction. Many of them gasped for breath and were stopped for rest breaks as we passed by. Eventually, we finished the 600 stairs and were back in the forested part of the woods. We were so glad we went down all those stairs instead of up!

Finally, we were back on a dirt trail and spent a few moments to appreciate the Poulanass Waterfall. It's a beautiful spot and a popular destination for visitors in the national park.

We continued the rest of the way down and followed the trail back to the visitor center.

It was a wonderful hike with stunning views all the way around. It was strenuous enough that we had the feeling of a great workout on an excellent trail.

This hike topped our list as one of our most enjoyable and favorites in Ireland.

ACKNOWLEDGEMENTS

Scott and I would like to thank all of our family and friends for their continued support of our hiking goals. Mimi Dimare, we appreciate you so much for taking care of our home and Joby, while giving him Mazey as a special friend.

A special thank you to Lou and Helen Bright, who if not for their stories of Ireland and greener pastures, we may not have been so inspired to explore Ireland.

As self-publishers, we couldn't do it without our editors and beta-readers, Shae Wall-Denzler and Jodi O'Keefe. You don't know how important it is for us to have fresh eyes on our work from people we can trust.

AUTHOR BIO

Scott and Jaynie wrote the active lifestyle travel blog, Backpacking Detours for three years. They have spent time in more than 25 countries; hiking, biking, food touring and drinking wine.

Their home is in the mountains of Northern California, where they own a heating and air-conditioning business. You will often find them training for their next long-distance hike.

Made in the USA
Columbia, SC
29 December 2019